GPS
for
Land Surveyors

Jan Van Sickle, PLS

Ann Arbor Press, Inc.
Chelsea, Michigan

Cover photograph by Trimble Navigation Ltd.

Library of Congress Cataloging-in-Publication Data

Catalog record is available from the Library of Congress.

ISBN 1-57504-041-7

ANN ARBOR PRESS, INC.
121 South Main Street, Chelsea, Michigan 48118

Printed in the United States of America
    5 6 7 8 9 0

To

Verna Van Sickle

About the Author

Jan Van Sickle, P.L.S. has 30 years experience as a land surveyor. He was privileged to supervise surveys with the first commercially available GPS receivers in the early 1980s and has worked with GPS ever since. He has taught at the Denver Institute of Technology and is a licensed surveyor in California, Colorado, and Oregon.

Preface

More than 20 years ago, GPS, the Global Positioning System was developed by the Department of Defense with military applications in mind. But today, it's the civilian users of the system that are stretching the limits of the technology. With the full constellation of GPS satellites, and the astonishing proliferation of GPS receivers, it is attracting users from every imaginable discipline.

Surveyors were there at the very beginning of GPS. They have known for a long time that GPS can measure latitude, longitude, altitude, velocity, and time with astonishing speed and accuracy. Still, most were kept out of the field by some pretty daunting obstacles, but those obstacles are finally falling away, one by one.

Cost: The GPS signal has always been free, but GPS hardware and software have certainly not been. Now the prices are falling, precipitously. And even as the costs go down, the capabilities of GPS receivers and processors are improving.

Convenience: When a precious few GPS satellites were up, they dictated the plan of observations, not the surveyor. And too often that schedule was not only expensive, but brutal for mere human beings. Today, with more than 22 usable satellites in orbit, 24-hour, worldwide service is a fact.

Applicability: The range of sizes, shapes, costs, and accuracies of GPS receivers is growing every year. And even that progress is exceeded by improvements in the software. GPS has a broader scope, shorter observation times, faster postmission processing and equipment with more capabilities than ever before.

The potential of GPS has always been great. What is new is the speed with which that potential has become reality. Even so, GPS is changing so fast, sometimes it's hard to know what questions to ask.

Many surveyors feel ill prepared for the use of GPS in their everyday work; the subject seems too complex; the time to digest it too long, and the books and seminars on the subject are either too complicated or oversimplified.

This book has been written to find a middle ground. It is an introduction to the concepts needed to understand and use GPS, not a presentation of the latest research in the area. An effort has been made to explain the progression of the ideas at the foundation of GPS.

This is also a practical book, a guide to some of the techniques used in the performance of a GPS survey. From its design through observation, processing, and troubleshooting, some of the aspects of a GPS survey are familiar to surveyors, some are not. This book is about making them all familiar.

Contents

Acronyms and Abbreviations

AOC	Auxiliary Output Chip
AODC	Age Of Data Clock
AODE	Age Of Data Ephemeris
AS	antispoofing
CDU	control and display unit
CIGNET	Cooperative International GPS Network
CIO	Conventional International Origin
CSOC	Consolidated Space Operations Center
CTP	Conventional Terrestrial Pole
CTS	Conventional Terrestrial System
DGPS	differential GPS; dynamic GPS
DOD	Department of Defense
DOP	dilution of precision
ECEF	earth-centered-earth-fixed
EDM	electronic distance measuring device
FGCC	Federal Geodetic Control Committee
GDOP	geometric dilution of precision
GPS	Global Positioning System
GRS80	Geodetic Reference System 1980
HARN	High Accuracy Reference Networks
HDOP	horizontal dilution of precision
HOW	handover word
Hz	hertz
IERS	International Earth Rotation Service
IGS	International GPS Geodynamics Service
IUGG	International Union of Geodesy and Geophysics
JPO	Joint Program Office
kHz	kilohertz
LF	low frequency
LLR	lunar laser ranging
Mbps	million bits per second
MCS	Master Control Station
MHz	megahertz
MIT	Massachusetts Institute of Technology
NAD83	North American Datum 1983

NASA	National Aeronautics and Space Administration
NAVSTAR	navigation system with timing and ranging
NGRS	National Geodetic Reference System
NGS	National Geodetic Survey
NGVD	National Geodetic Vertical Datums
NNSS	Navy Navigational Satellite System
NOAA	National Oceanic and Atmospheric Administration
OTF	on-the-fly
PDOP	position dilution of precision
PPS	Precise Positioning Service
PRN	pseudorandom noise
RA	right ascension
radar	radio detecting and ranging
RDOP	relative dilution of precision
RM	reference mark; reference monument
SA	selective availability
SLR	satellite laser ranging
SNR	signal-to-noise ratio
SPS	Standard Positioning Service
SV	space vehicle
TDOP	time dilution of precision
TLM	telemetry word
UERE	user equivalent range error
USC&GS	United States Coast and Geodetic Survey
USGS	United States Geological Survey
UTC	Coordinated Universal Time
UTM	Universal Transverse Mercator
VDOP	vertical dilution of precision
VHF	very high frequency
VLBI	very long baseline interferometry
WGS84	World Geodetic System 1984

Chapter One

The GPS Signal

GLOBAL POSITIONING SYSTEM (GPS) SIGNAL STRUCTURE

GPS and Trilateration

GPS can be compared to trilateration. Both techniques rely exclusively on the measurement of distances to fix positions. One of the differences between them, however, is that the distances, called ranges in GPS, are not measured to control points on the surface of the earth. Instead, they are measured to satellites orbiting more than 20,000 km above the earth.

A Passive System

The ranges are measured with signals that are broadcast from the GPS satellites to the GPS receivers in the microwave part of the electromagnetic spectrum; this is sometimes called a passive system. GPS is passive in the sense that only the satellites transmit signals; the users simply receive them. As a result, there is no limit to the number of GPS receivers that may simultaneously monitor the GPS signals. Just as millions of television sets may be tuned to the same channel without disrupt-

1

ing the broadcast, millions of GPS receivers may monitor the satellite's signals without danger of overburdening the system. This is a distinct advantage, certainly, but, as a result, GPS signals must carry a great deal of information. In essence, a GPS receiver must be able to gather all the information it needs to determine its own position strictly from the signals it collects from the satellites.

Time

Time directly affects GPS surveying in several ways. For example, the measurement of ranges, like the measurement of distances in a modern trilateration survey, is done electronically. In both cases, distance is a function of the speed of light, an electromagnetic signal of stable frequency and elapsed time. In a trilateration survey, a single clock within an electronic distance measuring device, EDM, can determine the elapsed travel time of its signal because the signal bounces off a reflector and returns to where it started. But the signals from a GPS satellite do not return to the satellite; they travel to the receiver and stop. A clock in the satellite can mark the moment the signal departs, and a clock in the receiver can mark the moment it arrives. Since, the measurement of the ranges in GPS depends on the measurement of the time it takes a GPS signal to make the trip from the satellite to the receiver, these two widely separated clocks communicate with each other. The GPS signal itself must carry the information that tells the receiver the exact time it left the satellite.

Control

Both GPS surveys and trilateration surveys begin from control points. In GPS, however, the control points are the satellites themselves; therefore, knowledge of the satellite's position is critical. In any type of surveying, the measurement of a distance to a control point without knowledge of that control point's position is useless. It is not enough that the GPS signals provide a receiver with information to measure the range between itself and the satellite. That same signal must also communicate the position of the satellite, at that very instant. The situation is complicated somewhat by the fact that the satellite is always moving. In a GPS survey, as in a trilateration survey, the signals must travel through the atmosphere. In a trilateration survey, compensation for the atmospheric effects on the EDM signal, estimated from local observations, can be applied at the signal's source. This is not possible in GPS. The GPS signals begin in the virtual vacuum of space, but then, after hitting the earth's atmosphere, they travel through much more of the atmosphere than most EDM signals. Therefore, the GPS signals must give the receiver some information about needed atmospheric corrections. It takes more than one measured distance to determine a new position in a trilateration survey or in a GPS survey. Each of the several distances used to define one new point must be measured to a different control station. For trilateration, three distances are adequate for each new point. In contrast, for a GPS survey the minimum requirement is a measured range to each of at least four GPS satellites. Just as it is vital that every one of the three distances in a trilateration is correctly paired with the correct station, the GPS receiver must be able to match each of the signals it tracks with the satellite of its origin. Therefore, the GPS signals themselves must also carry a kind of satellite identification. To be on the safe side, the signal should also tell the receiver where to find all of the other satellites as well.

To sum up, a GPS signal must somehow communicate to its receiver: (1) what time it is on the satellite, (2) the instantaneous position of a moving satellite, (3) some information about necessary atmospheric corrections, and (4) some sort of satellite identification system to tell the receiver where it came from and where the receiver may find the other satellites.

The Navigation Code

How does a GPS satellite communicate all that information to a receiver? It uses codes. Codes are carried to GPS receivers by two carrier waves. A carrier wave is a radio wave that has at least one characteristic that may be changed or modulated to carry information, such as phase, amplitude, or frequency. The two GPS carriers come from a part of the L-band. The L-band is a designation that includes all the radio frequencies from approximately 390 MHz to 1550 MHz.

Wavelength

A wavelength with a duration of 1 second, known as 1 cycle per second, is said to have a frequency of 1 hertz (Hz) in the International System of Units (SI). A frequency of 1 Hz is rather low. The lowest sound human ears can detect has a frequency of about 25 Hz. The highest is about 15,000 hertz, or 15 kilohertz (kHz).

Most of the modulated carriers used in EDMs and all those in GPS instruments have frequencies that are measured in units of a million cycles per second, or megahertz (MHz). The two fundamental frequencies assigned to GPS are called L1 at 1575.42 MHz and L2 at 1227.60 MHz.

Codes

GPS codes are binary, strings of zeroes and ones, the language of computers. The three basic codes in GPS are the precise code, or P code, the coarse/acquisition code, or C/A code, and the Navigation code. There are a few related secondary codes, which will be discussed later.

The Navigation code has a low frequency, 50 MHz, and is modulated onto both the L1 and L2 carriers. It communicates a stream of data called the GPS message, or Navigation message (Figure 1.1). This message is 1500 bits long, divided into five subframes with 10 words of 30 bits each. These subframes are the vehicles for telling the GPS receivers some of the most important things they need to know.

The accuracy of some aspects of the information included in the Navigation message deteriorates with time. Fortunately, mechanisms are in place to prevent the message from getting too old. The message is renewed each day by government uploading facilities around the world. These installations, along with their tracking and computing counterparts, are known collectively as the *Control Segment* (see Chapter 3).

GPS Time

One example of time-sensitive information is found in subframe 1 of the Navigation message. Using a standard time scale called *GPS Time*, the message contains information needed by the receiver to correlate its clock with that of the clock of the satellite. But the constantly changing time relationships in GPS can only be partially defined in this subframe. It takes more than a portion of the Navigation message to define those relationships. In fact, the rate of GPS Time is defined completely outside the system.

For example, the <u>rate</u> of GPS Time is kept within 1 microsecond of the <u>rate</u> of the worldwide time scale, which is called Coordinated Universal Time, UTC. The rate of UTC, determined by more than 150 atomic clocks located around the globe, is more stable than the rotation of the earth itself. This causes a discrepancy between UTC and the earth's actual motion. The difference is kept within 0.9 seconds by the periodic introduction of leap seconds in UTC. But since GPS is not earthbound, leap seconds are *not* used in GPS Time. This complicates the relationship between UTC and GPS Time. Even though their <u>rates</u> are virtually iden-

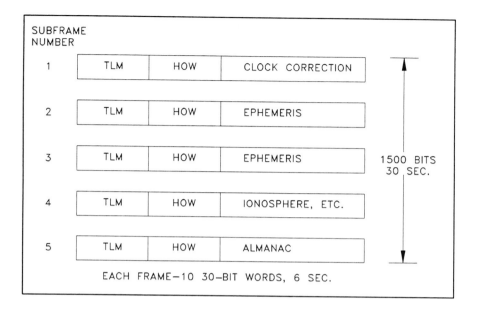

Figure 1.1. Navigation Message.

tical, an instant of time expressed in the GPS Time standard is different from the same instant expressed in UTC.

Satellite Clocks

Each GPS satellite carries its own onboard clocks in the form of four very stable and accurate atomic clocks regulated by the vibration frequencies of the atoms of two elements. Two of the onboard clocks are regulated by cesium and two are regulated by rubidium. Since the clocks in any one satellite are completely independent from those in any other, they are allowed to drift up to one millisecond from the strictly controlled GPS Time standard. Instead of constantly tweaking the satellite's onboard clocks to keep them all in lockstep with each other and with GPS Time, their individual drifts are carefully monitored by the government tracking stations of the Control Segment. These stations record each satellite clock's deviation from GPS Time. The drift is eventually uploaded into subframe 1 of each satellite's Navigation message, where it is known as the *broadcast clock correction*.

A GPS receiver may relate the satellite's clock to GPS Time with the correction given in the broadcast clock correction of its Navigation message. This is obviously only part of the solution to the problem of directly relating the receiver's own clock to the satellite's clock. The receiver will need to rely on other aspects of the GPS signal for a complete time correlation.

The drift of each satellite's clock is not constant. Nor can the broadcast clock correction be updated frequently enough to completely define the drift. Therefore, one of the 10 words included in subframe 1 provides a definition of the reliability of the broadcast clock correction. This is called AODC, or Age Of Data Clock.

Another example of time-sensitive information is found in subframes 2 and 3 of the Navigation message. They contain information about the position of the satellite, with respect to time. This is called the satellite's *ephemeris*.

The Broadcast Ephemeris

The satellite's ephemeris is given in a right ascension, RA, system of coordinates. These two subframes contain all the information the user's computer needs to calculate earth-centered, earth-fixed, WGS 84 coordinates of the satellite. The broadcast ephemeris, however, is far from perfect.

For example, the broadcast ephemeris is expressed in parameters that appear Keplerian. (Its elements are named for the 17th century German astronomer Johann Kepler.) But in this case, the appearance is deceiving. The GPS broadcast ephemeris parameters are not, strictly speaking, Keplerian at all. They are the result of least-squares, curve-fitting analysis of the satellite's actual orbit. Therefore, similarly to the broadcast clock correction, accuracy deteriorates with time. As a result, one of the most important parts of this portion of the Navigation message is called *AODE*. AODE is an acronym that stands for Age Of Data Ephemeris, and it appears in both subframe 2 and 3.

Atmospheric Correction

Subframe 4 addresses atmospheric correction. As with subframe 1, the data offer only a partial solution to a problem. The Control Segment's monitoring stations find the apparent delay of a GPS signal caused by its trip through the ionosphere through an analysis of the different propagation rates of the two frequencies broadcast by all GPS satellites, L1 and L2. These two frequencies and the effects of the atmosphere on the GPS signal will be discussed later. For now, it is sufficient to say that a single-frequency receiver can rely on the ionospheric correction in subframe 4 to help remove part of the error introduced by the atmosphere.

Antispoofing

Subframe 4 also contains a flag that tells the receiver when a security system, known as *antispoofing,* has been activated by the government ground control stations. At such times, the P code is replaced by the more secure Y code. Subframe 4 may also be asked to hold almanac information for satellites 25 through 32, should there be a need to increase the size of the constellation.

The Almanac

Subframe 5 tells the receiver where to find all the other GPS satellites. This subframe contains the ephemerides of up to 24 satellites, which is all the satellites in the current constellation. This is sometimes called *the almanac.* Here, the ephemerides are not complete. Their purpose is to help a GPS receiver lock onto more signals. Once the receiver finds its first satellite, it can look at the truncated ephemerides in subframe 5 of its Navigation message to figure the position of more satellites to track. But to collect any particular satellite's entire ephemeris, a receiver must acquire that satellite's signal and look there for subframes 2 and 3.

Satellite Health

Subframe 5 also includes *health data* for each satellite. GPS satellites are vulnerable to a wide variety of breakdowns, particularly clock trouble. That is one reason they each carry four clocks. Health data are also periodically uploaded by the ground control. Subframe 5 informs users of any satellite malfunctions before they try to use a particular signal.

Each of these five subframes begins with the same two words: the telemetry word TLM and the handover word HOW. Unlike nearly everything else in the Navigation message, these two words are generated by the satellite itself.

The TLM word is designed to indicate the status of uploading from the Control Segment while it is in progress. The HOW contains a number called the Z count, an important number for a receiver trying to acquire the P code, one of the primary GPS codes. The Z count tells the receiver exactly where the satellite stands in the generation of this very complicated code.

The P and C/A Codes

Similar to the Navigation message, the P and C/A codes are designed to carry information from the GPS satellites to the receivers. They, too, are impressed on the L1 and L2 carrier waves by modulation. However, unlike the Navigation message, the P and C/A codes are not vehicles for material uploaded by the ground control. They carry the raw data from which GPS receivers derive their time and distance measurements.

PRN

The P and C/A codes are complicated; so complicated, in fact, that they appear to be nothing but noise at first. Even though they are known as *pseudorandom noise,* or *PRN* codes, they are actually carefully designed. They have to be, because they must be capable of repetition and replication.

P Code

For example, the P code generated at a rate of 10.23 million bits per second is available on both L1 and L2. Each satellite repeats its portion of the P code every 7 days, and the entire code is renewed every 37 weeks. All GPS satellites broadcast their codes on the same two frequencies, L1 and L2. But a GPS receiver must somehow distinguish one satellite's transmission from another. One method used to facilitate this satellite identification is the assignment of one particular week of the 37-week-long P code to each satellite. For example, space vehicle 14 *(SV 14)* is so named because it broadcasts the fourteenth week of the P code.

C/A Code

The C/A code is generated at a rate of 1.023 million bits per second, 10 times slower than the P code. Here, satellite identification is quite straightforward. Not only does each GPS satellite broadcast a completely unique C/A code on its L1 frequency (and on L1 alone), but also the C/A code is repeated every millisecond.

SPS and PPS

The C/A code is the vehicle for the *SPS* (Standard Positioning Service), which is used for most civilian surveying applications. The P code, on the other hand, provides the same service for *PPS* (Precise Positioning Service). The current idea of SPS and PPS was developed by the Department of Defense. SPS is designed to provide a minimum level of positioning capability that is considered consistent with national security (at least ± 100 m), and can be intentionally degraded through *SA* (Selective Availability). PPS is designed for the highest positioning accuracy and is available only to users authorized by the Department of Defense.

The Production of a Modulated Carrier Wave

Since all the codes mentioned come to a GPS receiver on a modulated carrier, it is important to understand how a modulated carrier is generated. The signal created by an EDM is a good example of a modulated carrier.

EDM Ranging

As mentioned earlier, an EDM only needs one clock because its electromagnetic wave travels to a retroprism and is reflected back to its origination. The EDM is both the transmitter and the receiver of the signal. Therefore, in general terms, the instrument can take half the time elapsed between the moment of transmission and the moment of reception, multiply by the speed of light, and find the distance between itself and the retroprism (Distance = Elapsed Time × Rate).

Illustrated in Figure 1.2, the fundamental elements of the calculation of the distance measured by an EDM, ρ, are the time elapsed between transmission and reception of the signal, Δt, and the speed of light, c.

$$\text{Distance} = \rho$$

$$\text{Elapsed Time} = \Delta t$$

$$\text{Rate} = c.$$

GPS Ranging

However, the one-way ranging used in GPS is more complicated. It requires the use of two clocks. The broadcast signals from the satellites are collected by the receiver, not reflected. Nevertheless, in general terms, the full time elapsed between the instant a GPS signal leaves a satellite and arrives at a receiver, multiplied by the speed of light, is the distance between them.

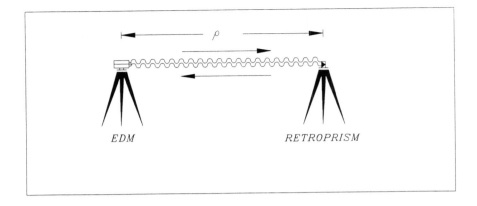

Figure 1.2. Two-Way Ranging.

Unlike the wave generated by an EDM, a GPS signal cannot be analyzed at its point of origin. The measurement of the elapsed time between the signal's transmission by the satellite and its arrival at the receiver requires two clocks, one in the satellite and one in the receiver. This complication is compounded because these two clocks must be perfectly synchronized with one another. Since such perfect synchronization is a physical impossibility, the problem is addressed mathematically.

In Figure 1.3, the basis of the calculation of a range measured from a GPS receiver to the satellite, ρ, is the multiplication of the time elapsed between a signal's transmission and reception, Δt, by the speed of light, c. However, a discrepancy of 1 microsecond between the clock aboard the GPS satellite and the clock in the receiver can create a range error of 300 meters, far beyond the acceptable limits for nearly all surveying work.

Oscillators

Although they are called clocks, the time measurement devices used in both EDM and GPS measurements are more correctly called oscillators, or *frequency standards*. In other words, they don't produce a steady series of ticks. They keep time by chopping a continuous beam of electromagnetic energy at extremely regular intervals. The result is a steady series of wavelengths and the foundation of the modulated carrier.

For example, the action of a shutter in a movie projector is analogous to the modulation of a coherent infrared beam by the oscillator in an EDM. Consider the visible beam of light passing through a movie projector. It is interrupted by the shutter, half of a metal disk rotating at a constant rate

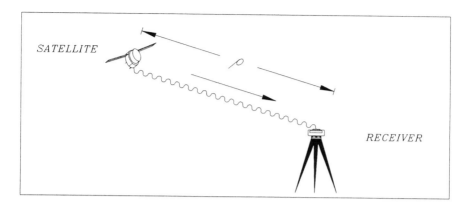

Figure 1.3. One-Way Ranging.

that alternately blocks and uncovers the light. In other words, the shutter chops the continuous beam into equal segments by virtue of its stable rotation. Each length begins with the shutter closed and the light beam entirely blocked. As the shutter rotates open, the light beam is gradually uncovered. It increases to its maximum intensity, and then decreases again as the shutter gradually closes. The light is not simply turned on and off, it gradually increases and decreases.

This modulation can be illustrated by a sine wave (Figure 1.4). The wavelength begins when the light is blocked by the shutter. The first minimum is called a 0° *phase angle*. The first maximum is called the 90° phase angle and occurs when the shutter is entirely open. It returns to minimum at the 180° phase angle when the shutter closes again. But the wavelength isn't yet complete. It continues through a second shutter opening, 270°, and closing, 360°. The 360° phase angle marks the end of one wavelength and the beginning of the next one. The time and distance between every other minimum; that is, from the 0° to the 360° phase angles, is a wavelength and is usually symbolized by the greek letter lambda, λ.

As long as the rate of an oscillator's operation is very stable, both the length and elapsed time between the beginning and end of every wavelength will be the same.

A Chain of Electromagnetic Energy

GPS oscillators are sometimes called clocks because the frequency of a modulated carrier, measured in hertz, can indicate the elapsed time be-

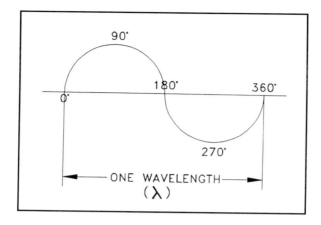

Figure 1.4. 0° to 360° = 1 wavelength.

tween the beginning and end of a wavelength, which is a useful bit of information for finding the distance covered by a wavelength. The length is approximately:

$$\lambda = \frac{c_a}{f}$$

Where: λ = the length of each complete wavelength in meters
c_a = the speed of light corrected for atmospheric effects
f = the frequency of the modulated carrier in hertz

For example, if an EDM transmits a carrier with a modulating frequency of 9.84 MHz and the speed of light is approximately 300,000,000 meters per second (a more accurate value is 299,792,458 meters per second, but the approximation 300,000,000 meters per second will be used here for convenience), then:

$$\lambda = \frac{c_a}{f}$$

$$\lambda = \frac{300,000,000 \; mps}{9,840,000 \; Hz}$$

$$\lambda = 30.49 \; m$$

the modulated wavelength would be about 30.49 meters long, or approximately 100 feet.

Using the same formula, the L1-1575.42 MHz radio frequency transmitted by GPS satellites has a wavelength of approximately 19 cm.

$$\lambda = \frac{c_a}{f}$$

$$\lambda = \frac{300 \times 10^6 \ mps}{1575.42 \times 10^6 \ Hz}$$

$$\lambda = 0.19 \ m$$

The L2-1227.60 MHz frequency transmitted by GPS satellites has a wavelength of approximately 24 cm.

$$\lambda = \frac{c_a}{f}$$

$$\lambda = \frac{300 \times 10^6 \ mps}{1227.60 \times 10^6 \ Hz}$$

$$\lambda = 0.24 \ m$$

A Chain of Electromagnetic Energy

The modulated carrier transmitted from an EDM can be compared to an ultramodern Gunter's chain constructed of electromagnetic energy instead of wire links. Each full link of this electromagnetic chain is a wavelength of a specific frequency. The measurement between an EDM and a reflector is doubled with this electronic chain because, after it extends from the EDM to the reflector, it bounces back to where it started. The entire trip represents twice the distance, and is simply divided by 2 to reveal the desired measurement. Like the surveyors who used the old Gunter's chain, one cannot depend on a particular measurement to conveniently end at the beginning or the end of a complete link (or wavelength). A measurement is much more likely to end at some fractional part. The question is, where?

Phase Shift

With the original Gunter's chain, the surveyor simply looked at the chain and estimated the fractional part of the last link that should be included in the measurement. However, those links were tangible. Since the wavelengths of a modulated carrier are not tangible, the EDM must find the fractional part of its measurement electronically. Therefore, it does a comparison. It compares the phase angle of the returning signal to that of a replica of the transmitted signal to determine the phase shift. That *phase shift* represents the fractional part of the measurement. This principle is used in distance measurement by both EDM and GPS systems.

How does it work? First, it is important to remember that points on a modulated carrier are defined by phase angles, such as 0°, 90°, 180°, 270°, etc. (Figure 1.4). When two modulated carrier waves reach exactly the same phase angle at exactly the same time, they are said to be *in phase, coherent,* or *phase locked.* However, when two waves reach the same phase angle at different times, they are *out of phase* or *phase shifted.* For example, in Figure 1.5, the sine wave shown in the dashed line has returned to an EDM from a reflector. Compared with the sine wave shown in the solid line, it is out of phase by one-quarter of a wavelength. The distance between the EDM and the reflector, ρ, is then:

$$\rho = \frac{(n\lambda + d)}{2}$$

where: n = the number of full wavelengths the modulated carrier has
completed
d = the fractional part of a wavelength at the end that completes the doubled distance.

In this example, d is three-quarters of a wavelength. But how would the EDM know that?

It knows because at the same time an external carrier wave is sent to the reflector, the EDM keeps an identical internal reference wave at home in its receiver circuits. When the external beam returns from the reflector, it is compared to this reference wave and the difference in phase between the two is measured (see Figure 1.6).

Both EDM and GPS ranging use the measurement represented in this illustration. In GPS, the measurement of the difference in the phase of the incoming signal and the phase of the internal oscillator in the receiver

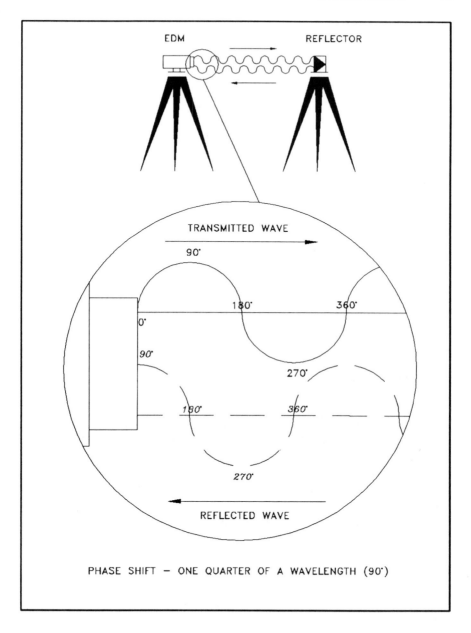

Figure 1.5. An EDM Measurement.

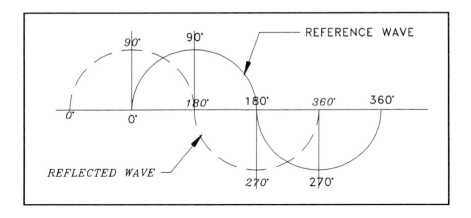

Figure 1.6. Reference and Reflected Waves.

reveals the small distance at the end of a range. In GPS, the process is called *carrier phase ranging.*

The Cycle Ambiguity Problem

While this technique discloses the fractional part of a wavelength, the problem remains of determining the number of full wavelengths of the modulated carrier between the transmitter and the receiver. This cycle ambiguity problem is sometimes solved in EDM measurements by modulating the carrier in ever-longer wavelengths. For example, the meter and part of a meter aspects of a measured distance can be resolved by measuring the phase difference of a 10 meter wavelength. This procedure may be followed by the resolution of the tens of meters using a wavelength of 100 meters. The hundreds of meters can then be resolved with a wavelength of 1000 meters, and so on. Such a method is convenient for the EDM's two-way ranging system, but is impossible in the one-way ranging used in GPS measurements.

GPS ranging must use an entirely different strategy for solving the cycle ambiguity problem because the satellites broadcast only two constant wavelengths, in one direction, from the satellites to the receivers. Unlike an EDM measurement, the wavelengths of the modulated carriers in GPS cannot be changed to resolve the number of cycles between transmission and reception. Nevertheless, the carrier phase measurements remain an important *observable* in GPS ranging.

TWO OBSERVABLES

The word *observable* is used throughout GPS literature to indicate the signals whose measurement yields the range or distance between the satellite and the receiver. The word is used to draw a distinction between the thing being measured, the observable, and the measurement, the observation.

There are two types of observables: the *pseudorange* and the carrier phase. The latter, also known as the *carrier beat phase*, is the basis of the techniques used for high-precision GPS surveys. On the other hand, the pseudorange can serve applications when virtually instantaneous point positions are required or relatively low accuracy will suffice.

These basic observables can also be combined in various ways to generate additional measurements that have certain advantages. It is in this latter context that pseudoranges are used in most GPS receivers as a preliminary step toward the final determination of position by carrier phase measurement.

The foundation of pseudoranges is the correlation of code carried on the signal received from a GPS satellite with a replica of that code generated in the receiver.

Most of the GPS receivers used for surveying applications are capable of code correlation; that is, they can determine pseudoranges from the C/A code or the P code. These same receivers are usually capable of determining ranges using the carrier phase as well. However, first let us concentrate on the C/A code that is impressed on the carrier and that make pseudorange measurements possible.

Phase Modulation

The GPS carriers L1 and L2 could have been modulated in a variety of ways: amplitude, frequency, or phase modulations. But the C/A and P codes impressed on the GPS carriers are the result of phase modulations. One consequence of this modulation is that the signal occupies a broader bandwidth than it would otherwise. The GPS signal is said to have a *spread spectrum* because of its intentionally increased bandwidth. This characteristic offers several advantages, including more accurate ranging, increased security, and less interference.

The particular kind of phase modulation used in GPS is known as *binary biphase* modulation, in which each zero and one of the binary code is known as a *code chip*. Zero represents the *normal* state, and one represents the *mirror image* state. In other words, the frequency and amplitude of the carrier remains constant while the modulations from zero to one and from one to zero are accomplished by instantaneous 180° changes in phase. Note in Figure 1.7 that each shift from zero to one, and from one to zero, is accompanied by a corresponding change in the phase of the carrier.

The rate of all of the components of GPS signals are multiples of the standard rate of the oscillators, 10.23 MHz. This rate is known as the *fundamental clock rate* and is symbolized F_o. For example, the GPS carriers are 154 times F_o, or 1575.42 MHz, and 120 times F_o, or 1227.60 MHz, L1 and L2, respectively.

The codes are also based on F_o. 10.23 *code chips* of the P code, zeros or ones, occur every microsecond. In other words, the *chipping rate* of the P code is 10.23 million bits per second, 10.23 Mbps, exactly the same as F_o, 10.23 MHz.

The chipping rate of the C/A code is 10 times slower than the P code, a tenth of F_o, 1.023 Mbps. Ten P code chips occur in the time it takes to generate one C/A code chip, allowing P code derived pseudoranges to be 10 times more precise; this is one reason the C/A code is known as the *coarse/acquisition code.*

Even though both codes are broadcast on L1, they are distinguishable from one another by their transmission in *quadrature*. That means that the C/A code modulation on the L1 carrier is phase-shifted 90° from the P code modulation on the same carrier.

PSEUDORANGING

Strictly speaking, a pseudorange observable is based on a time shift. This time shift can be symbolized by $d\tau$, d tau, and is the time elapsed between the instant a GPS signal leaves a satellite and the instant it arrives at a receiver. The concept can be illustrated by the process of setting a watch from time signals heard over a telephone.

Propagation Delay

Imagine that a recorded voice said, "The time at the tone is 3 hours and 59 minutes." If it were possible to set a watch to that time at the instant the tone was heard, the watch would certainly be slow. It would be slow because at the moment the tone was broadcast, the time was 3 hours and 59 minutes but the moment the tone was <u>heard</u>, the time was a bit later. It is later by the time it took for the tone to travel through the telephone lines from the point of broadcast to the point of reception. This elapsed time would be equal to the length of the circuitry traveled by the

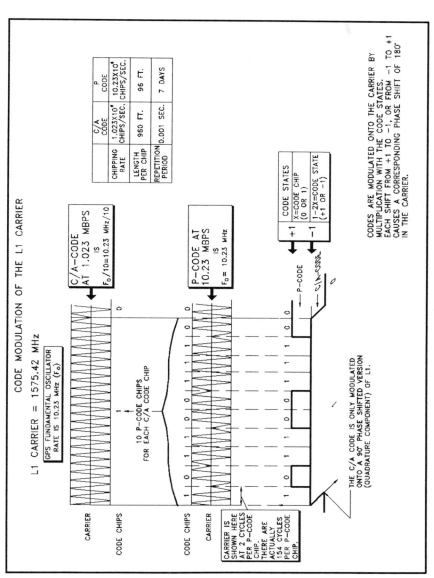

Figure 1.7. Code Modulation of the L1 Carrier.

tone divided by the speed of the electricity, which is the same as the speed of all electromagnetic energy, including light and radio signals.

In GPS, that extra time is known as the *propagation* delay. The measurement of this very small delay is accomplished by a combination of the GPS codes. However, the idea is very similar to the strategy used in EDMs. Similar to an EDM that generates an internal replica of its carrier wave to correlate with the signal it receives by reflection, a GPS receiver generates a replica *code* that it can correlate with the code it receives directly from the satellite.

Code Correlation

To conceptualize the process, one can imagine two codes generated at precisely the same time and identical in every regard: one in the satellite and one in the receiver. The satellite sends its code to the receiver but on its arrival, the two codes don't line up. Though the codes are identical, they don't *correlate* until the replica code in the receiver is time-shifted in relation to the satellite code to accommodate the propagation delay—then they match perfectly. Under ideal circumstances, the time shift required would be exactly the time it took for the satellite code to travel down to the receiver. Unfortunately, there are environmental and physical limitations on the process that prevent such a simple relationship.

Autocorrelation

Actually lining up the code from the satellite with the replica in the GPS receiver is called *autocorrelation* and is dependent on the transformation of code chips into *code states*. The formula used to derive code states (+1 and −1) from code chips (0 and 1) is:

$$\text{code state} = 1 - 2x$$

where x is the code chip value. For example, a normal code state is +1 and corresponds to a code chip value of 0. The mirror code state is −1 and corresponds to a code chip value of 1.

The function of these code states can be illustrated by asking two questions. If a tracking loop of 10 replica code states that is generated in a receiver does not match 10 code states from the satellite, how does the receiver know? Second, how does the receiver know when a tracking loop of 10 replica code states does match 10 code states from the satellite? The answer to the first question is that when the codes do not match, the sum of the products of each code state of the replica 10, with each of the 10 from the satellite, divided by 10, is *not 1*. The answer to the second question is that when the codes do match, the sum of the products of each code state of the replica 10, with each of the 10 from the satellite, divided by 10, is *exactly 1*.

The *autocorrelation function* is:

$$\frac{1}{N}\int_0^T X(t)*X(t-\tau)dt = \frac{1}{N}\sum_{i=1}^N X_i * X_{i-j}$$

In Figure 1.8, before the code from the satellite and the replica from the receiver are matched, the sum of the products of the code states is less than 1:

$$\frac{1}{10}\sum_{i=1}^{10} X_i * X_i - 4 = \frac{1}{10}(+1+1+1-1-1+1+1+1-1+1) = +0.40$$

Following the correlation of the two codes, the sum of the code states is exactly 1.:

$$\frac{1}{10}\sum_{i=1}^{10} X_i * X_i = \frac{1}{10}(+1+1+1+1+1+1+1+1+1+1) = +1.0$$

Lock and the Time Shift

Once correlation of the two codes is achieved, it is maintained within the GPS receiver. If the correlation is somehow destroyed later, the receiver is said to have *lost lock*. However, as long as the lock is present, the Navigation message is available to the receiver.

The Navigation message is the previously mentioned 50 MHz code impressed onto both carriers with the other codes. Its broadcast clock corrections relating the satellite's onboard clocks with GPS time can now be combined with the described code correlation to estimate the actual time shift called the *pseudorange*.

It would be wonderful if the time shift $d\tau$, d tau, discovered in the correlation of the satellite code with the replica code could be multiplied by the speed of light to find the true range, ρ, of the satellite. However, such a straightforward measurement of this elapsed time would require, among other things, that the clock in the satellite and

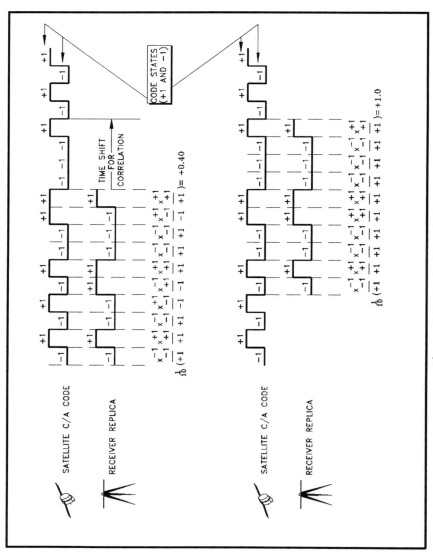

Figure 1.8. Code Correlation.

the clock in the receiver be perfectly synchronized with each other, which is an impossibility.

Imperfect Oscillators

Actually, if the satellite clock and the receiver clocks (oscillators) are checked against the carefully controlled GPS Time, they can be seen to be wandering constantly. Their oscillators are imperfect, and those in the satellites are subject to the further destabilizing effects of drastic changes in temperature, acceleration, and radiation. These inconsistencies, along with others, bias every range measurement. That is one reason they are called a pseudoranges.

A Pseudorange Equation

Clock offsets are not the only errors in pseudoranges. There are several others. Their relationship can be illustrated by the following equation (Langley, 1993):

$$p = \rho + c(dt - dT) + d_{ion} + d_{trop} + \epsilon_p$$

where:
p	=	the pseudorange measurement
ρ	=	the true range
c	=	the speed of light
dt	=	the satellite clock offset from GPS Time
dT	=	the receiver clock offset from GPS Time
d_{ion}	=	ionospheric delay
d_{trop}	=	tropospheric delay
ϵ_p	=	multipath and receiver noise.

Please note that the pseudorange, p, and the true range, ρ, are not equivalent without consideration of clock offsets, atmospheric effects, and other biases.

But this discussion should not lose sight of the real objective, which is finding the position of the receiver. If the coordinates of the satellite and the coordinates of the receiver were known perfectly, it would, of course, be a simple matter to determine time shift, $d\tau$, and find the true range, ρ, between them.

In fact, it can be useful to imagine that the true range term, ρ, also known as the *geometric range*, actually includes the coordinates of both the satellite and the receiver. However, they are hidden within the measured value, the pseudorange p, along with all of the other terms on the right side of the equation. The objective, then, is to mathematically separate and quantify these biases so the receiver coordinates can be revealed. Clearly, any deficiency in describing, or *modeling*, the biases will degrade the quality of the final determination of the receiver's position (see Figure 1.9).

The One-Percent Rule of Thumb

A pseudorange can be resolved to approximately 1 percent of the chipping rate of the code used, whether it is the P code or the C/A code. A P code chip occurs every 0.0978 of a microsecond. Therefore, a P code based pseudorange measurement can have a precision of about 1 percent of a tenth of a microsecond, or 1 nanosecond. One nanosecond multiplied by the speed of light is approximately 30 centimeters, 1 percent of the length of a single P-code chip.

The C/A code based pseudorange is 10 times less precise. Its chipping rate is 10 times slower. A C/A code pseudorange has a precision of about 3 meters, 1 percent of the length of a single C/A code chip.

This one-percent rule of thumb is often used in GPS to illustrate the increased precision of the carrier phase observable over the pseudorange. A carrier phase measurement can be resolved to approximately 1 percent of the wavelength of the L1 carrier, or about 2 millimeters.

A 3-meter ranging precision is not adequate for most land surveying applications. Carrier phase observations are certainly the preferred method for the higher-precision work most surveyors have come to expect from GPS.

CARRIER PHASE RANGING

Carrier Phase Comparisons

Carrier phase is the GPS observable at the center of surveying applications of GPS. The carrier phase measurement depends on the carrier waves themselves, the unmodulated L1 and L2, instead of their P and C/A codes. One bit of good news is apparent from this strategy: the user is probably immune from SA, selective availability. As mentioned earlier, SA is the intentional degradation of the standard positioning service (SPS) available through the C/A code. Since carrier phase observations do not use codes, they are not affected by SA.

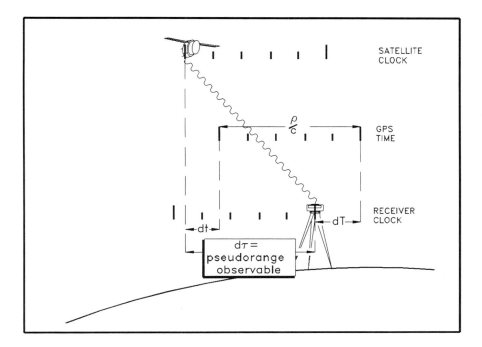

Figure 1.9. Pseudorange.

Carrier phase is perhaps a bit more difficult to manage than the pseudorange, but the basis of the measurements has some similarities. For example, the foundation of a pseudorange measurement is the correlation of the codes received from a GPS satellite with replicas of those same codes generated within the receiver. Similarly, the foundation of the carrier phase measurement is the combination of the carrier received from a GPS satellite with a replica of that carrier generated within the receiver.

Phase Difference

A few similarities can also be found between a carrier phase observation and a distance measurement by an EDM. As mentioned earlier, an EDM sends an external carrier wave to the reflector and generates an identical internal reference carrier. When the external beam returns from the reflector, it is compared to the reference wave. The difference in phase between the two reveals the fractional part of the measurement, even though the number of complete cycles is not immediately known.

Likewise, the difference in the phase of an incoming signal with the phase of the internal reference reveals the fractional part of the carrier phase measurement in GPS. The incoming signal is from a satellite rather than a reflector, but, like an EDM measurement, the internal reference is derived from the receiver's own oscillator, and the number of complete cycles is not immediately known.

Beat

The carrier phase observable is sometimes called the *reconstructed carrier phase* or *carrier beat phase* observable. In this context, a *beat* is the pulsation resulting from the combination of two waves with different frequencies. An analogous situation occurs when two musical notes of different pitch are sounded at the same time. Their two frequencies combine and create a third note, called the *beat*. Musicians can tune their instruments by listening for the beat that occurs when two pitches differ slightly. This third pulsation may have a frequency equal to the difference, or the sum of the two original frequencies.

The beat phenomenon is by no means unique to musical notes. It can occur when any pair of oscillations with different frequencies are combined. In GPS, a beat is created when a carrier generated in a GPS receiver and a carrier received from a satellite are combined. At first, that might not seem sensible. How could a beat be created by combining two absolutely identical carriers? After all, there should not be a difference in frequency between an L1 carrier generated in a satellite and an L1 carrier generated in a receiver. They both should have a frequency of 1575.42 MHz. If there is no difference in the frequencies, how can there be a beat? Because there is a difference between the two carriers. Something happens to the frequency of the carrier on its trip from a GPS satellite to a receiver: its frequency changes. The phenomenon is described as the Doppler effect.

The Doppler Effect

Again, sound provides a model for the explanation of the behavior of radio waves. An increase in the frequency of a sound is indicated by a rising pitch; a lower pitch is the result of a decrease in the frequency. A stationary observer listening to the blasting horn on a passing train notices that the pitch rises as the train gets closer and falls as the train travels away. Furthermore, the change in the sound, which is clear to the observer standing beside the track, is not heard by the engineer driving the train. He hears only one constant, steady pitch. The relative motion of the train with respect to the observer causes the apparent variation in the frequency of the sound of the horn.

In 1842, Christian Doppler used an analogy of a ship on an ocean with equally spaced waves to describe the frequency shift named for him. When the ship is stationary, the waves strike it steadily, one each second. But, if the ship sails into the waves, they break across its bow more frequently. If the ship then turns around and sails with the waves, they strike less frequently across its stern. The waves themselves have not changed; in fact, their frequency is constant. However, to the observer on the ship, their frequency appears to depend on the direction of the ship's travel. When the ship sails against the waves, their frequency appears to increase. When the ship sails with the waves, their frequency appears to decrease.

GPS and the Doppler Effect

From the observer's point of view, it does not matter whether it is the source, the observer, or both that are moving. The frequency increases while they move together and decreases while they move apart. Therefore, if a GPS satellite is moving toward an observer, its carrier comes into the receiver with a higher frequency than it had when it left the satellite. If a GPS satellite is moving away from the observer, its carrier comes into the receiver with a lower frequency than it had at the satellite. Since a GPS satellite is always moving with respect to the observer, any signal received from a GPS satellite is Doppler-shifted.

Carrier beat phase, then, is the phase of the signal created by the difference of this incoming Doppler-shifted satellite carrier with the nominally constant carrier frequency generated by the receiver's oscillator (Figure 1.10).

Conventional Notations

In GPS literature, the carrier phase observation (in cycles) is often symbolized by *phi*, ϕ. Other conventions include the use of superscripts to indicate satellite designations and the use of subscripts to define receivers. For example, in the following equation ϕ_r^s is used to symbolize the carrier phase observation between satellite, *s*, and receiver, *r*. The difference that defines the carrier beat phase observation is (Wells, 1986):

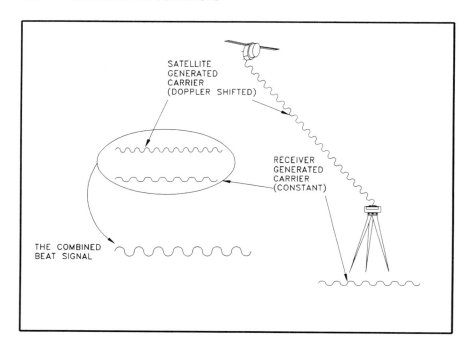

Figure 1.10. The Carrier Beat Phase.

$$\phi = \phi_r^s = \phi^s(t) - \phi_r(T)$$

$\phi^s(t)$ is the phase of the carrier broadcast from the satellite, *s*, at time, *t*. Note that the frequency of this carrier is the same nominally constant frequency that is generated by the receiver's oscillator; $\phi_r(T)$ is its phase when it reaches the receiver *r* at time *T*.

A description of the use of the carrier phase observable to measure range can start with the same basis as the calculation of the pseudorange, travel time. The time elapsed between the moment the signal is broadcast, *t*, and the moment it is received, *T*, multiplied by the speed of light, *c*, will yield the range between the satellite and receiver, ρ:

$$(T - t)c \approx \rho$$

Using this simplified equation, it is possible to arrive at an approximate idea of the relation between time and range for some assumed nominal values. These values could not be the basis of any actual carrier phase observation because, among other reasons, it is not possible for the receiver to know when a particular carrier wave left the satellite. For the purpose of illustration, suppose a carrier left a satellite at 00 hr 00 min 00.000 sec, and arrived at the receiver 75 milliseconds later.

$$(T - t)c \approx \rho$$

$$00h{:}00m{:}00.075s - 00h{:}00m{:}00.000s)\ 300{,}000 km\ /\ s \approx \rho$$

$$(0.075)300{,}000 km\ /\ s \approx \rho$$

$$22{,}500 km \approx \rho$$

This estimate indicates that if the carrier broadcast from the satellite reaches the receiver 75 milliseconds later, the range between them is approximately 22,500 km, about midway between the apogee and perigee of the NAVSTAR GPS satellites.

Carrying this example a bit farther, the wavelength, λ, of the L1 carrier can be calculated by dividing the speed of light, c, by the L1 frequency, f:

$$\lambda = \frac{c}{f}$$

$$\lambda = \frac{300{,}000{,}000\ m\ /\ s}{1{,}575{,}420{,}000\ Hz}$$

$$\lambda = 0.1904254104\ m$$

Dividing the approximated range, ρ, by the calculated L1 carrier wavelength, λ, yields a rough estimation of the carrier phase in cycles, ϕ:

$$\frac{\rho}{\lambda} \approx \phi$$

$$\frac{22{,}500{,}000\ m}{0.1904254104\ m} \approx \phi$$

$$118{,}156{,}500\ cycles \approx \phi$$

The 22,500-km range implies that the L1 carrier would cycle through approximately 118,156,500 wavelengths on its trip from the satellite to the receiver.

Carrier Phase Biases

Of course, these relationships are simplified. However, they can be made fundamentally correct by recognizing that ranging with the carrier phase observable is subject to the same biases and errors as the pseudorange. For example, terms such as the receiver clock offset may be incorporated, again symbolized by dT, as it was in the pseudorange equation. The imperfect satellite clock can be included, its error is symbolized by dt. The tropospheric delay, d_{trop}, the ionospheric delay, d_{ion}, and multipath and receiver noise, ϵ_ϕ, are also added to the range measurement. The ionospheric delay will be negative here, and that will be discussed later. With these changes, the simplified travel time equation can be made a bit more realistic:

$$[(T+dT)-(t+dt)]c = \rho - d_{ion} + d_{trop} + \epsilon_\phi$$

This more realistic equation can be rearranged to isolate the elapsed time, *(T-t)*, on one side, by dividing both sides by c, and then moving the clock errors to the right side (Wells, 1986).

$$\frac{[(T+dT)-(t+dT)]c}{c} = \frac{\rho - d_{ion} + d_{trop} + \epsilon_\phi}{c}$$

$$[(T+dT)-(t+dt)] = \frac{\rho - d_{ion} + d_{trop} + \epsilon_\phi}{c}$$

$$(T-t+dT-dt) = \frac{\rho - d_{ion} + d_{trop} + \epsilon_\phi}{c}$$

$$(T-t+dT-dt)+(dt-dT) = \frac{\rho - d_{ion} + d_{trop} + \epsilon_\phi}{c} + (dt-dT)$$

$$T-t = dt-dT + \frac{\rho - d_{ion} + d_{trop} + \epsilon_\phi}{c}$$

This expression now relates the travel time to the range. Unfortunately, a carrier phase observation cannot rely solely on the travel time for two reasons. First, in a carrier phase observation the receiver has no codes with which to tag any particular instant in time on the incoming continuous carrier wave. Second, since the receiver cannot distinguish one cycle of the carrier from any other, it has no way of knowing the initial phase of the signal when it left the satellite. The result of these difficulties is that the receiver cannot know the signal's actual travel time and, therefore, the receiver cannot determine the number of complete cycles between the satellite and itself. This unknown number, the complete cycles between a satellite and a receiver, is an integer called the *cycle ambiguity*. The approximation of a cycle ambiguity calculated earlier (118,156,500 wavelengths) was for the purpose of comparison and illustration only. In actual practice, a carrier phase observation must derive the range from a measurement of phase at the receiver, not from a given signal's travel time.

The critical unknown integer, the cycle ambiguity, is symbolized by N. It cannot be measured directly by the receiver. Even though the receiver can count the complete phase cycles it receives from the moment it starts tracking until the moment it stops, and although it can measure the fractional phase cycles, the cycle ambiguity, N, remains unknown.

An Illustration of the Cycle Ambiguity Problem

The situation is somewhat analogous to an unofficial technique used by some nineteenth-century contract surveyors on the Great Plains. This old procedure, known as the buggy wheel method of chaining can be used as a rough illustration of the cycle ambiguity problem in GPS. Some of the lines of the public land system that crossed open prairies were originally surveyed by loading a buckboard wagon with stones or stakes and tying a cloth to a spoke of the wheel. One man drove the team. Another kept the wagon on line with a compass. A third counted the revolutions of the flagged wheel to measure the distance. When there had been enough turns of the improvised odometer to measure half a mile, they set a stone or stake to mark the corner and then rolled on, counting their way to the next corner.

A GPS receiver is the man assigned to count the turns of the wheel. He is supposed to begin his count from the moment the crew leaves the newly set corner. Instead, suppose he jumps into the wagon, gets comfortable and takes an unscheduled nap. When he awakens, the wagon is on the move, and trying to make up for his laxness, he immediately begins counting the revolutions of the wheel. At that instant, the wheel is at a half turn, a fractional part of a cycle, so he counts the subsequent half turn. Then, back on the job, he studiously counts each and every full turn of the wheel. His tally grows as the cycles accumulate, but he is in trouble and he knows it. He has no real idea of how far the wagon has traveled because he was asleep for the first part of the trip. He has no way of knowing how many times the wagon wheel turned before he woke up and started counting. He is like a GPS receiver that cannot know how far it is from the satellite when it starts counting phase cycles. The number of full and fractional wheel revolutions he counts now can tell him nothing about how many cycles occurred while he was asleep. It is like the count of phase cycles by a GPS receiver, a count that can tell nothing about how many cycles stood between the receiver and the satellite when the receiver was switched on and began tracking. Those unknown cycles are the cycle ambiguity, N, and it can be discovered in GPS.

REFERENCES

Langley, R.B. "The GPS Observables," in *GPS World,* 4(4):52–59 (1993).
Wells, D., Ed. *Guide to GPS Positioning,* Fredericton, New Brunswick: Canadian GPS Associates (1986).

Chapter Two

Biases and Solutions

THE ERROR BUDGET

A Look at the Biases in the Observation Equations

The management of errors is indispensable for finding the true geometric range ρ from either a pseudorange, or carrier phase observation.

$$p = \rho + c(dt - dT) + d_{ion} + d_{trop} + \in_p \quad (pseudorange)$$

$$\phi = \rho + c(dt - dT) + \lambda N - d_{ion} + d_{trop} + \in_\phi \quad (carrier\ phase)$$

Both equations include environmental and physical limitations called *range biases*.

The Biases

Among these biases are certain atmospheric errors; two such errors are the ionospheric delay, d_{ion}, and the tropospheric delay, d_{trop}. The tropospheric delay may be somewhat familiar to EDM users, if the ionospheric delay is not. Other biases, clock errors symbolized by *(dt − dT)*

33

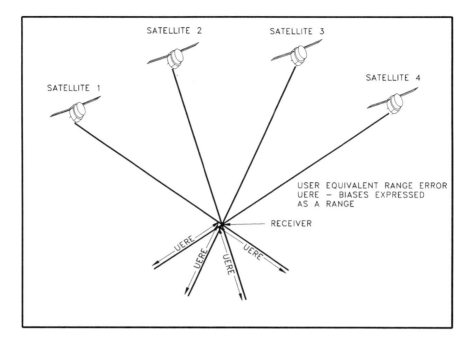

Figure 2.1. User Equivalent Range Error.

and receiver noise, multipath, etc., (combined in the symbols $\in_p$ and $\in_\phi$) are unique to satellite surveying methods. The objective here is to mathematically separate and quantify each of these biases.

UERE

When each bias is expressed as a range itself, each quantity is known as a *user equivalent range error* or *UERE*. This expression, often used in GPS literature, is a convenient way to clarify the individual contributions of each bias to the overall biased range measurement (Figure 2.1). The UERE of the biases common to both the pseudorange and carrier phase equations will be used here to present a sense of their relative sizes and the conditions that govern their magnitudes.

The Satellite Clock Bias, *dt*

The largest error can be attributed to the satellite clock bias. A range error as large as 300 km can occur if the broadcast clock correction is **not** used by the receiver to bring the time signal acquired from a satellite's onboard clock in line with GPS Time.

Satellite Clock Drift

As discussed in the Chapter 1, the onboard satellite clocks are independent of one another. Since the rates of these rubidium and cesium oscillators are more stable if they are not disturbed by frequent tweaking, adjustment is kept to a minimum. They are allowed to drift up to a millisecond from GPS Time.

By constantly monitoring the satellite's clock error, dt, the Control Segment gathers data for its daily uploads of the broadcast clock corrections. The primary purpose of these corrections is to reduce the potential UERE from 300 km with 1 millisecond of satellite clock error, to around 10 meters, by bringing the satellite's clock within about 30 nanoseconds of GPS time. You will recall that clock corrections are part of the Navigation message; more specifically, part of subframe 1 of that message.

The Ionospheric Effect, d_{ion}

The relatively unhindered travel of the GPS signal through the virtual vacuum of space changes as it passes through the earth's atmosphere. Through both refraction and diffraction, the atmosphere alters the apparent speed and, to a lesser extent, the direction of the signal.

Group and Phase Delay

The ionosphere is the first layer the signal encounters. It extends from about 50 km to 1000 km above the earth's surface. Traveling through this layer of the atmosphere the most troublesome effects on the GPS signal are known as the *group delay* and the *phase delay*. They both alter the measured range. The magnitude of these delays is determined by the density and stratification of the ionosphere at the moment the signal passes through it.

TEC

The density of the ionosphere changes with the number and dispersion of free electrons released by the ionization of its gas molecules by the sun's ultraviolet radiation. This density is often described as *total electron content* or *TEC,* a measure of the number of free electrons in a column through the ionosphere with a cross-sectional area of 1 square meter.

Ionosphere and the Sun

The relationship between the density of the ionosphere and the sun's activity is clear in the midlatitudes. For example, during the daylight hours the ionospheric delay may be as much as five times greater than it is at night. It is also nearly four times greater in November, when the earth is nearing its closest approach to the sun, its *perihelion,* than it is in July near the earth's *aphelion,* its farthest point from the sun. The effect of the ionosphere on the GPS signal usually reaches its peak in March, about the time of the vernal equinox.

Ionospheric Gradients

The ionosphere is not homogeneous. It changes from layer to layer within a particular area. Its behavior in one region of the earth is liable to be unlike its behavior in another. For example, ionospheric disturbances can be particularly harsh in the polar regions. But the highest TEC values and the widest variations in the horizontal gradients of the ionosphere occur in the band of about 60° of *geomagnetic latitude*, lying 30° north and south of the earth's magnetic equator.

The disturbances in the ionosphere in the equatorial region have a severity not seen in the midlatitudes. In that area, refraction and diffraction peak from sunset to midnight. Their effect may become severe enough to cause GPS receivers to lose lock.

Satellite Elevation and Ionospheric Effect

Another factor in the severity of the ionospheric effect is the amount of time the GPS signal spends traveling through the layer. A signal originating from a satellite near the observer's horizon must pass through a larger amount of the ionosphere to reach the receiver than does a signal from a satellite near the observer's zenith. The longer the signal is in the ionosphere, the greater the ionosphere's effect, and the greater the impact of horizontal gradients within the layer.

The Magnitude of the Ionospheric Delay

Although the error introduced by the ionosphere can be as small as 5 m or less in some instances, the ionospheric effect can nonetheless contribute the second largest UERE in others. It may be as large as 150 meters when the satellite is near the observer's horizon; the vernal equinox is near and sunspot activity is at the maximum of its 11-year cycle. But the ionospheric effect varies with magnetic activity, location, time of day, and even observing direction.

The Ionosphere Affects Codes and the Carrier Wave Differently

Fortunately, the ionosphere has a property that can be used to minimize its effect on GPS signals. It is *dispersive*. The length of the apparent time delay contributed by the ionosphere depends on the frequency of the signal. One result of this dispersive property is that during the signal's trip through the ionosphere the modulations on the carrier wave of the GPS signal are affected differently than the carrier wave itself.

The ionospheric delay can be divided into two distinct categories: *phase delay* and *group delay*. All the modulations on the carrier wave, the P code, the C/A code, and the Navigation message, appear to be slowed. They are affected by the group delay. But the carrier wave itself appears to speed up in the ionosphere. It is affected by the phase delay.

It may seem odd to call an increase in speed a delay, but, governed by the same properties of electron content as the group delay, phase delay merely increases negatively. Note that the algebraic sign of d_{ion} is negative in the carrier phase equation and positive in the pseudorange equation.

Different Frequencies Are Affected Differently

Another consequence of the *dispersive* nature of the ionosphere is that the apparent time delay for a higher frequency carrier wave is less than it is for those with a lower frequency. That means that L2 is not affected as much as L1. This fact leads to one of the greatest advantages of a dual-frequency receiver over the single-frequency receivers. By tracking both carriers, a dual-frequency receiver has the facility of modeling and removing not all, but a significant portion of the ionospheric bias.

The frequency dependence of the ionospheric effect is described by the following expression, (Klobuchar, 1983 in Brunner and Welch, 1993).

$$v = \frac{40.3}{cf^2} \cdot TEC$$

where v =   the ionospheric delay
      c =   the speed of light in meters per second
      f =   the frequency of the signal in Hz
   TEC =   the quantity of free electrons per cubic meter.

As the formula illustrates, the time delay is inversely proportional to the square of the frequency. The higher the frequency, the less the delay, and hence the dual-frequency receiver's capability to discriminate the effect on L1 from that on L2. Such a dual-frequency model can usually be used to reduce the UERE to the decimeter level. Still, it is far from perfect and cannot ensure the effect's elimination.

Broadcast Correction

As mentioned in Chapter 1, an ionospheric correction is also available to the single frequency receiver in subframe 4 of the Navigation message. However, this broadcast correction should not be expected to remove more than about three-quarters of the ionospheric effect.

The Receiver Clock Bias, dT

The third largest error can be caused by the receiver clock error. A UERE from 100 meters to 10 meters may be attributed to receiver clock error, depending on the oscillator type. Both a receiver's measurement of phase differences and its generation of replica codes depend on the reliability of its internal frequency standard, its oscillator.

Typical Receiver Clocks

GPS receivers are usually equipped with quartz crystal clocks which are relatively inexpensive and compact. They have low power requirements and their 10-year lifespan compares favorably to the 5-year life of cesium and rubidium oscillators. For these types of clocks, the frequency is generated by the piezoelectric effect in an oven-controlled quartz crystal disk, a device sometimes symbolized by $OCXO$. Their reliability ranges from a minimum of about 1 part in 10^8 to a maximum of about 1 part in

10^{10}. The latter is a magnitude about equal to a quarter of a second over a human lifetime. Even at that, quartz clocks are not as stable as the atomic standards in the GPS satellites and are more sensitive to temperature changes, shock, and vibration. Some receiver designs augment their frequency standards by also having the capability to accept external timing from cesium or rubidium oscillators.

The Orbital Bias

Orbital bias has the potential to be the fourth largest UERE, but this ephemeris-based bias is not symbolized in the observation equations at all. It is addressed in the broadcast ephemeris.

Forces Acting on the Satellites

The orbital motion of GPS satellites is not only a result of the earth's gravitational attraction, but also several other forces that act on the satellite. The primary disturbing forces are the nonspherical nature of the earth's gravity, the attractions of the sun and the moon, and solar radiation pressure. The best data available to model these forces are the actual motion of the satellites themselves and this tracking is accomplished by government facilities distributed around the world, known collectively as the *Control Segment.*

Tracking Facilities

The Master Control Station *MCS* is located at the Consolidated Space Operations Center *CSOC* at Falcon Air Force Base in Colorado Springs, Colorado. This station computes updates for the Navigation message, generally, and the broadcast ephemeris, in particular, from about one week of tracking information it collects from five monitoring stations around the world. Every GPS satellite is tracked by at least one of these monitoring stations at all times and the orbital tracking data gathered by monitoring stations are then passed on to the Master Control Station. There, new ephemerides are computed. This tabulation of the anticipated locations of the satellites with respect to time is then transferred to four uploading stations, where it is transmitted back to the satellites themselves.

Unfortunately, there are some difficulties in the process of updating the satellite's orbital information. The broadcast ephemeris must be a prediction, since it is based on the satellite's past behavior. The Control

Segment's forecasting capability is hampered further by an incomplete understanding of the precise nature of the forces acting on the satellites.

Broadcast Ephemeris

The broadcast ephemeris is not valid for a satellite's entire orbit, since it is the result of least-squares curve fitting of the predicted ephemeris over a few hours of the satellite's path. Therefore, a particular satellite's position can only be calculated to an accuracy of about 20 meters, with occasional errors as large as 80 meters.

The Tropospheric Effect, d_{trop}

The fifth largest UERE can be attributed to the effect of the troposphere.

Troposphere

The troposphere is that part of the atmosphere closest to the earth. In fact, it extends from the surface to about 9 km over the poles and 16 km over the equator, but in this work it will be combined with the tropopause and the stratosphere, as it is in much of GPS literature. Therefore, the following discussion of the tropospheric effect will include the layers of the earth's atmosphere up to about 50 km above the surface.

Tropospheric Effect Is Independent of Frequency

Like the ionospheric effect, the tropospheric delay appears to add a slight distance to the range the receiver measures between itself and the satellite. But the troposphere and the ionosphere are by no means alike in their effect on the satellite's signal. The troposphere is *nondispersive* for frequencies below 30 GHz. In other words, the refraction of a GPS satellite's signal is not related to its frequency in the troposphere.

The troposphere is part of the *electrically neutral* layer of the earth's atmosphere, meaning it is neither ionized nor dispersive. Therefore, both L1 and L2 are equally refracted. Like the ionosphere, the density of the troposphere also governs the severity of its effect on the GPS signal. For example, when a satellite is close to the horizon, the delay of the signal caused by the troposphere is maximized, whereas the tropospheric delay of the signal from a satellite at zenith, directly above the receiver, is minimized.

Satellite Elevation and Tropospheric Effect

The situation is analogous to atmospheric refraction in astronomic observations; the effect increases as the energy passes through more of the atmosphere. The difference in GPS is that it is the delay, not the angular deviation, caused by the changing density of the atmosphere that is of primary interest. The GPS signal that travels the shortest path through the troposphere will be the least delayed by it. So, even though the delay at an elevation angle of 90° will only be about 2.4 meters, it increases to about 9.3 meters at 75° and 20 meters at 10°.

Modeling

Modeling the troposphere is one technique used to reduce the bias in GPS data processing, and it can be up to 95 percent effective. However, the residual 5 percent can be quite difficult to remove. For example, surface measurements of temperature and humidity are not strong indicators of conditions on the path between the receiver and the satellite. But instruments that can provide some idea of the conditions along the line between the satellite and the receiver are somewhat more helpful in modeling the tropospheric effect.

The Dry and Wet Components of Refraction

Refraction in the troposphere has a dry component and a wet component. The dry component is closely correlated to the atmospheric pressure and can be more easily estimated than the wet component. It is fortunate that the dry component contributes the larger portion of range error in the troposphere, since the high cost of water vapor radiometers and radiosondes generally restricts their use to only the most high-precision GPS work.

Receiver Spacing and the Atmospheric Biases

There are other practical consequences of the atmospheric biases. For example, the character of the atmosphere is never homogeneous, and the importance of atmospheric modeling increases as the physical distance between GPS receivers grows. Consider a signal traveling from one satellite to two receivers that are close together. That signal would be subjected to very similar atmospheric effects, and, therefore, atmospheric bias modeling would be less important to the accuracy of the measurement between them. But a signal traveling from the same satellite to two receivers that are far apart would pass through levels of atmosphere quite different from one another. In that case, atmospheric bias modeling would be more important.

Multipath

The range delay known as *multipath,* included in the symbols $\in_p$ and $\in_\phi$, differs from both the apparent slowing of the signal through the ionosphere and troposphere and the time differences caused by clock offsets. The range delay in multipath is the result of the reflection of the GPS signal.

Multipath occurs when part of the signal from the satellite reaches the receiver after reflecting from the ground, a building, or another object. One or more of these reflected signals can then interfere with the signal that reaches the receiver directly from the satellite.

Limiting the Effect of Multipath

The high frequency of the GPS codes tends to limit the field over which multipath can contaminate pseudorange observations. Once a receiver has achieved lock; that is, its replica code is correlated with the incoming signal from the satellite, signals outside the expected chip length can be rejected. Multipath signals that are delayed by their reflection so that they travel an additional distance of more than about 1½ times the typical chip length are ignored by the receiver. For example, a P code chip is 29.3 meters long; a multipath signal that is behind the direct signal by 44 meters or so will not disrupt the receiver. Similarly, a C/A code chip is 293 meters long; the receiver will reject a multipath signal that is 440 meters or so behind the direct signal. However, multipath signals that have delays smaller than 1½ times the chip length will still contaminate the pseudorange measurement.

A multipath error of 3 meters or more in range can result from a reflected P coded signal that travels just 18 meters or 20 meters more than the signal arriving directly from the satellite. The same 3 meters of range error can result from a reflected C/A coded signal that travels 180 meters or 200 meters behind the direct signal.

There are other factors that distinguish reflected multipath signals from direct signals. For example, reflected signals at the frequencies used for L1 and L2 tend to be more diffuse than the directly received signals. Another difference involves the circular polarization of the GPS signal. The polarization is actually reversed when the signal is reflected. These characteristics allow some multipath signals to be identified and rejected at the receiver's antenna.

Antenna Design and Multipath

GPS antenna design can play a role in minimizing the effect of multipath. Ground planes, usually a metal sheet of about a square meter or so, are used with many antennas to reduce multipath interference by eliminating signals from low elevation angles, while other antennas have gain patterns that are null at low elevations. The most widely used strategy is the 15° cutoff or *mask angle*. This technique calls for tracking satellites only after they are more than 15° above the receiver's horizon. Careful attention in placing the antenna away from reflective surfaces, such as nearby buildings or vehicles, is another way to minimize the occurrence of multipath.

DIFFERENCING

Classifications of Positioning Solutions

Kinematic GPS

Speaking broadly, there are two applications of GPS in surveying and geodesy, *kinematic* and *static* positioning. Kinematic applications imply movement, one or more GPS receivers actually in motion during their observations. A moving platform, a vehicle on land, sea, or air, equipped with a GPS receiver, is characteristic of kinematic GPS. Other characteristics of the application include results in real time and little redundancy. Hydrography, aerial mapping, and gravimetric surveying use kinematic GPS.

Static GPS

Static applications use observations from receivers that are stationary for the duration of their measurement. Despite some recent advances in real-time work on short lines, most static applications have the advantage of postmission processing and can afford higher redundancy than kinematic GPS. The majority of GPS surveying and geodetic work relies on static applications.

Hybrid Techniques in GPS

There have been recent hybrids between kinematic and static applications. *Pseudokinematic* and *semikinematic* rely on short static observations and, in the first instance, revisits to positions once occupied; in the second, the alternate movement of multiple receivers. Another hybrid is called *rapid static*. The receivers used in rapid static are stationary during their observations, but their observations are very short, and they rely on both code and carrier observations on both L1 and L2.

Relative and Point Positioning

Kinematic and static applications include two classifications, *point positioning* and *relative positioning*; in other words, there are four possible combinations. They are: *static point positioning, static relative positioning, kinematic point positioning,* and *kinematic relative positioning*. Generally speaking, static positioning is more accurate than kinematic, and relative positioning is more accurate than point positioning.

The term *differential* GPS, or *DGPS*, has come into common usage as well. Use of this acronym usually indicates a method of relative positioning where coded pseudorange measurements are used rather than carrier phase.

Point Positioning

Point positioning is virtually the only technique possible when a lone GPS receiver is available. The simplest type of point positioning can be represented by a single receiver measuring its range from a single satellite (Figure 2.2). Using pseudorange measurements, this technique is subject to all of the biases represented in the pseudorange equation. (Note: the range symbol in this illustration can be "p" rather than "ρ")

$$p = \rho + c(dt - dT) + d_{ion} + d_{trop} + \in_p$$

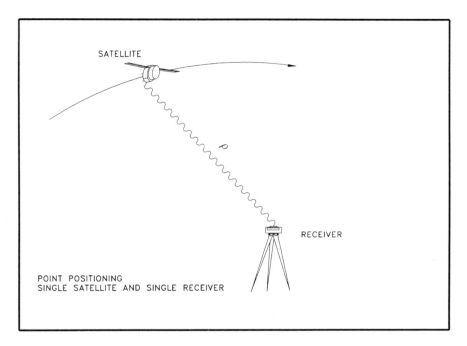

Figure 2.2. Point Positioning.

Biases in Point Positioning

The atmospheric correction available in the Navigation message is assumed correct, as is the broadcast ephemeris. The timing errors between the receiver and satellite clocks, receiver noise, and any multipath still contaminate the result. (See the section titled, "The Error Budget," for a more complete discussion of these biases.)

In using this method, the combined UEREs would probably be less than the sum of the biases, and some could be minimized by modeling. However, even the minimum magnitudes of these biases make this kind of point positioning unacceptable for most surveying applications.

The Navigation Solution

Another type of point positioning is known as *absolute positioning*, *single-point positioning* or *the Navigation solution*. It is characterized by a single receiver measuring its range to four satellites simultaneously (Figure 2.3). Four satellites is the minimum requirement for this type of solution, but the more satellites, the better the derived position.

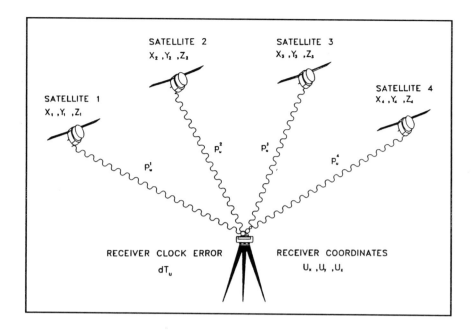

Figure 2.3. Navigation Solution.

The Navigation solution is in one sense the fulfillment of the original idea behind GPS. It relies on a coded pseudorange measurement and can be used for virtually instantaneous positioning.

In this method, the positions of the satellites are available from the data in their broadcast ephemerides. The satellite clock offset and the ionospheric correction are also available from the Navigation messages of all four satellites.

Four Unknowns

Even if all these data are presumed to contain no errors, which they surely do, four unknowns remain: the position of the receiver in three Cartesian coordinates, u_x, u_y, and u_z, and the receiver's clock error dT_u. Three pseudoranges provide enough data to solve for u_x, u_y, and u_z. And the fourth pseudorange provides the information for the solution of the receiver's clock offset.

$$p_u^1 = \sqrt{(X^1 - u_x)^2 + (Y^1 - u_y)^2 + (Z^1 - u_z)^2} + c(dT_u)$$

$$p_u^2 = \sqrt{(X^2 - u_x)^2 + (Y^2 - u_y)^2 + (Z^2 - u_z)^2} + c(dT_u)$$

$$p_u^3 = \sqrt{(X^3 - u_x)^2 + (Y^3 - u_y)^2 + (Z^3 - u_z)^2} + c(dT_u)$$

$$p_u^4 = \sqrt{(X^4 - u_x)^2 + (Y^4 - u_y)^2 + (Z^4 - u_z)^2} + c(dT_u)$$

(Note: the range symbols in these equations <u>must</u> be "p" rather than "ρ," since these ranges include all the range biases. As it says it Chapter 1, "p is the pseudorange measurement and ρ is the true range.")

The ability to achieve so much redundancy in the measurement of the dT is one reason the moderate stability of quartz crystal clock technology is entirely adequate as a receiver oscillator.

Four Satellites and Four Equations

A unique solution is found here because the number of unknowns is not greater than the number of observations. The receiver tracks four satellites simultaneously; therefore, these four equations are solved simultaneously for every *epoch* of the observation. An epoch in GPS is a very short period of observation time, and is generally just a small part of a longer measurement. However, theoretically there is enough information in any single epoch of the Navigation solution to solve these equations. In fact, the trajectory of a receiver in a moving vehicle could be determine by this method. With four satellites available, resolution of a receiver's position and velocity are both available through the simultaneous solution of these four equations. These facts are the foundation of the kinematic application of GPS.

Relative Positioning

Correlation

The availability of two or more GPS receivers makes relative positioning possible. Relative positioning can attain higher accuracy than point positioning because of the extensive correlation between observations taken to the same satellites at the same time from separate stations. Because the distance between such stations on the earth are short compared with the 20,000-km altitude of the GPS satellites, two receivers operating simultaneously, collecting signals from the same satellites will record very similar errors.

Baselines

The vectors between such pairs of receivers are known as *baselines*. The simultaneity of observation, the resulting error correlation, and the carrier phase observable, combine to yield baseline measurements accuracies from 1 ppm to 0.1 ppm.

Networks

Network or *multireceiver positioning* are obvious extensions of relative positioning. Both the creation of a closed network of points by combining individually observed baselines and the operation of three or more receivers simultaneously have advantages. For example, the baselines have redundant measurements and similar, if not identical, range errors. The processing methods in such an arrangement can nearly eliminate many of the biases introduced by imperfect clocks and the atmosphere. These processing strategies are based on computing the differences between simultaneous GPS carrier phase observations.

Differencing

In GPS, the word *differencing* has come to represent several types of simultaneous baseline solutions of combined measurements. The most frequently used are known as the *single difference, double difference,* and *triple difference.*

Single Difference

One of the foundations of differencing is the idea of the baseline as it is used in GPS. For example, a single difference, also known as a *between-receivers difference*, can refer to the difference in the simultaneous carrier phase measurements from one GPS satellite as measured by two different receivers (Figure 2.4).

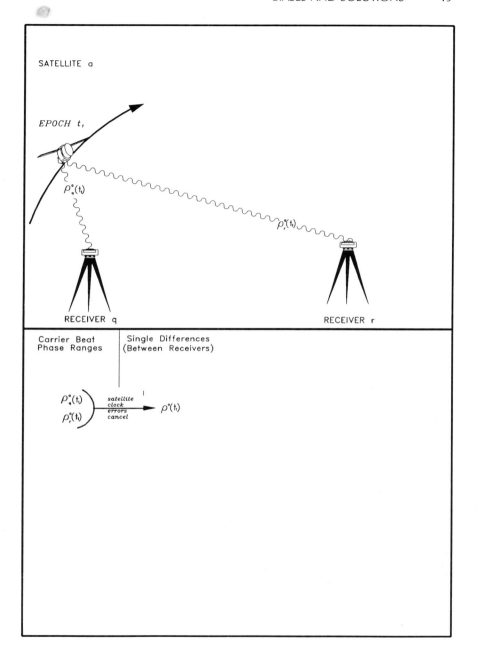

Figure 2.4. Carrier Phase Measurements from One GPS Satellite as Measured by Two Different Receivers.

Elimination of the Satellite Clock Errors

In this single-difference solution, the satellite clock error is eliminated. The difference between dt at the first receiver and dt at the second receiver, Δdt, is zero. Since the two receivers are both observing the same satellite at the same time, the satellite clock bias is canceled out. The atmospheric biases and the orbital errors recorded by the two receivers in this solution are nearly identical, so they, too, can also be virtually eliminated.

Other Errors Remain

Unfortunately, there are still two factors in the carrier beat phase observable that are not eliminated by single differencing. The difference between the integer cycle ambiguities at each receiver, ΔN, and the difference between the receiver clock errors, ΔdT, remain.

Double Difference

Elimination of the Receiver Clock Errors

There is a GPS solution that will eliminate the receiver clock errors. It involves the addition of what might be called another kind of single difference, also known as a *between-satellites difference*. This term refers to the difference in the carrier beat phase measurement of signals from two GPS satellites, as measured simultaneously at a single receiver (Figure 2.5).

The data available from the between-satellites difference allow the elimination of the receiver clock error. In this situation, there can be no difference in the clock, since only one is involved. And the atmospheric effects on the two satellite signals are again nearly identical as they come into the lone receiver, so the effects of the ionospheric and tropospheric delays are virtually eliminated as well.

No Clock Errors At All

By using both the between-receivers difference and the between-satellites difference, a double difference is created. This double difference contains no clock errors whatsoever. Both the receiver clock and satellite clock errors are canceled out completely.

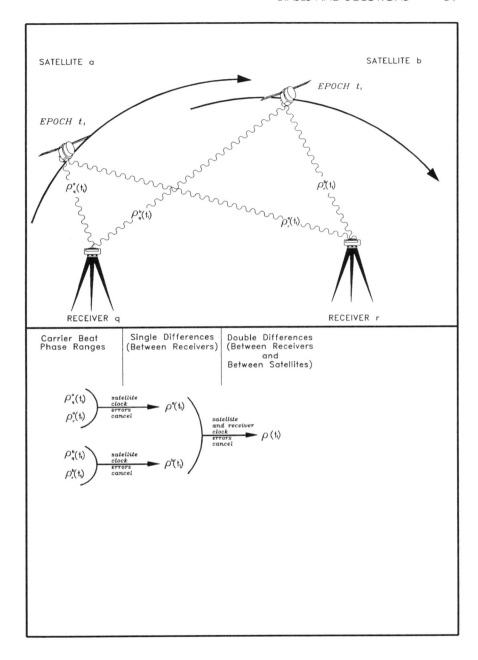

Figure 2.5. Carrier Beat Phase Measurement from Two GPS Satellite, as Measured at a Single Receiver.

Triple Difference

A third kind of differencing is created by combining two double differences. Each of the double differences involves two satellites and two receivers. The difference next derived is between two epochs. The triple difference is also known as the *receiver-satellite-time triple difference* (Figure 2.6).

Elimination of the Cycle Ambiguity

In the triple difference, two receivers observe the same two satellites during two consecutive epochs. This solution eliminates the integer cycle ambiguity, N, because if all is as it should be, N is constant over the two observed epochs. Therefore, the triple difference makes the detection and elimination of cycle slips relatively easy.

Cycle Slips

A *cycle slip* is a discontinuity in a receiver's continuous phase lock on a satellite's signal. The coded pseudorange measurement is immune from this difficulty, but the carrier beat phase is not.

Components of the Carrier Phase Observable

From the moment of a receiver's lock onto a particular satellite, there are actually three components to the total carrier phase observable.

$$\phi = \alpha + \beta + N$$

where: ϕ = total phase
α = fractional initial phase
β = observed cycle count
N = cycle count at lock on

Fractional Initial Phase

First is the *fractional initial phase* which occurs at the receiver at the first instant of the lock-on. Then the receiver starts following the incoming phase from the satellite without knowing what instant of time would

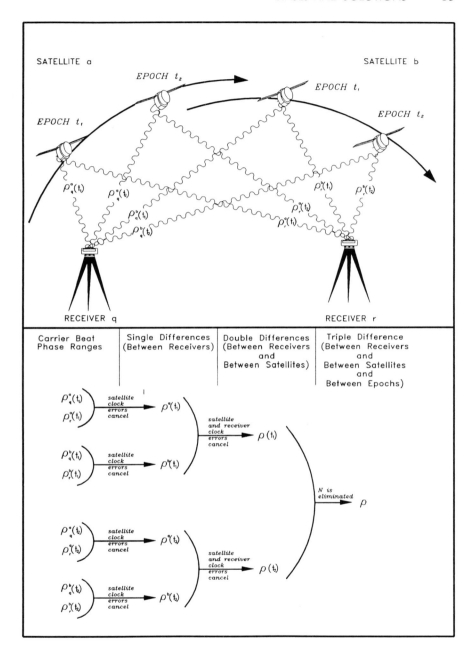

Figure 2.6. The Receiver-Satellite-Time Triple Difference.

afford a perfect synchronization. Lacking this knowledge, the receiver grabs onto the satellite's signal at some fractional part of a phase, rather than the beginning of a wavelength. This fractional part does not change for the duration of the observation, and so is called the fractional initial phase. It is symbolized here by α.

The Integer Number of Cycles

Second is the integer number of full cycles of phase that occur from the moment of the lock to the end of the observation. It is symbolized here by β and labeled as the observed cycle count. This element is tantamount to the receiver's consecutively counting full phase cycles, 1, 2, 3, 4 . . ., as the range changes between the receiver and the satellite because of the satellite's relative movement with respect to the receiver. Of the three, it is only this number that changes smoothly—that is, if the observation proceeds correctly.

The Cycle Ambiguity

Third is the integer cycle ambiguity, N. It represents the number of full phase cycles between the receiver and the satellite at the first instant of the receiver's lock-on. It is labeled as the cycle count at lock-on. N does not change from the moment of the lock onward, unless that lock is lost.

Lost Lock

When lock is lost, a cycle slip occurs. A power loss, an obstruction, a very low signal-to-noise ratio, or any other event that breaks the receiver's continuous reception of the satellite's signal causes a cycle slip. That is, the receiver loses its place in its count of the integer number of cycles β and, as a result, N is completely lost.

Finding and Fixing Cycle Slips

There are several methods that may be used to regain a lost integer phase value, N. The triple difference is one of the better alternatives in this regard. A triple difference is not affected by any type of clock errors. Therefore, when a large residual appears in its component double differences after the receiver's position has been determined, it is very likely that it is caused by a cycle slip. The obstructed signal can be singled-out by isolating all available satellite pairs until the discontinuity is found. It is this utility in fixing cycle slips that is the primary appeal of the triple difference.

Summary

Typical Techniques

Relative positioning by carrier beat phase measurement is the primary vehicle for GPS surveying. Simultaneous static observations, double differencing in postprocessing, and the subsequent construction of networks from GPS baselines are the hallmarks of the majority of the work in the field. The strengths of these methods generally outweigh their weaknesses, particularly where there can be an unobstructed sky and relatively short baselines, and where the length of observation sessions is not severely restricted.

Pseudorange and Carrier Phase

However, conditions are not always so ideal. Where obstructions threaten to produce cycle slips, coded pseudorange measurements may offer an important advantage over carrier beat phase. Pseudorange measurements also may be preferred where accuracy requirements are low and production demands are high.

Kinematic GPS

There can hardly be a question that kinematic GPS is the most productive of the several alternative methods, under the right circumstances. However, the necessity of maintaining lock on four or more satellites as the receiver is moved, currently limits its application to very open areas.

Other Techniques

Rapid-static, pseudokinematic, and other hybrid methods are attempts to take advantage of some of the best aspects of static positioning, such as high accuracy and predictable production, while improving on its drawbacks. It is almost always desirable to increase production by employing shorter observation sessions, provided it can be done while maintaining the required accuracy.

Differencing

Differencing is an ingenious approach to minimizing the effect of errors in carrier beat phase ranging. Double differencing, the most widely used formulation, makes the very highest accuracy possible with GPS.

Biases

However, in this discussion of errors it is important to remember that multipath, cycle slips, incorrect instrument heights, and a score of other errors whose effects can be minimized or eliminated by good practice are simply not within the purview of differencing at all. The unavoidable biases that can be managed by differencing—including clock, atmospheric, and orbital errors—can have their effects drastically reduced by the proper selection of baselines, the optimal length of the observation sessions, and several other considerations included in the design of a GPS survey. But such decisions require an understanding of the sources of these biases and the conditions that govern their magnitudes. The adage of, "garbage in, garbage out," is as true of GPS as any other surveying procedure. The management of errors cannot be relegated to mathematics alone.

Next Chapter

In the next chapter, the forerunners of GPS are presented. It is often said that GPS is new. In fact, GPS is more than two decades old, and the principles of satellite positioning were developed long before the appearance of the Global Positioning System. Therefore, some of the aspects of GPS are more easily understood when they are placed in the context of their origins.

REFERENCE

Brunner, F.K. and W.M. Welsch, "Effect of the Troposphere on GPS Measurements," in *GPS World,* 4(1):42–51 (1993).

Chapter Three

The Framework

TECHNOLOGICAL FORERUNNERS

Consolidation

In the early 1970s the Department of Defense, DOD, commissioned a study to define its future positioning needs. That study found nearly 120 different types of positioning systems in place, all limited by their special and localized requirements. The study called for consolidation, and NAVSTAR GPS (navigation system with timing and ranging, global positioning system) was proposed. Specifications for the new system were developed to build on the strengths and avoid the weaknesses of its forerunners. Here is a brief look at the earlier systems and their technological contributions toward the development of GPS.

Terrestrial Radio Positioning

Radar

Long before the satellite era, the developers of *radar* (radio detecting and ranging) were working out many of the concepts and terms still used in electronic positioning today. For example, the classification of the radio portion of the electromagnetic spectrum by arbitrary letters, such as the L band now used in GPS, was introduced during World War II to maintain the secrecy of radar research. Even the concept of measuring distance with electromagnetic signals (ranging in GPS) had one of its earliest practical applications in radar; since then there have been several incarnations of the idea.

Distance by Timing

Shoran (short range navigation), a method of electronic ranging using pulsed *VHF* (very high frequency) signals, was originally designed for bomber navigation, but was later adapted to more benign uses. The system depended on a signal, sent by a mobile transmitter-receiver-indicator unit being returned to it by a fixed transponder. The elapsed time of the round trip was then converted to distances.

Shoran Surveying

It wasn't long before the method was adapted for use in surveying. Using shoran from 1949 to 1957, Canadian geodesists were able to achieve precisions as high as 1:56,000 on lines of several hundred kilometers. Shoran's success led to the development of *Hiran* (high-precision Shoran). Its pulsed signal was more focused, its amplitude more precise, and its phase measurements more accurate.

Hiran Surveying

Hiran, also applied to geodesy, was used to make the first connection between Africa, Crete, and Rhodes in 1943. But its most spectacular application were the arcs of triangulation joining the North American Datum 1927 with the European Datum 1950 in the early '50s. By knitting together continental datums, Hiran might be considered to be the first practical step toward positioning on a truly global scale.

Sputnik

These and other radio navigation systems proved that ranges derived from accurate timing of electromagnetic radiation were viable. But useful as they were in geodesy and air-navigation, they only whet the a petite oor l hirhergplaifora. In 1957, the development of Sputnik, the first earth-orbiting satellite, made that possible.

Some of the benefits of earth-orbiting satellites soon became clear. The potential coverage was virtually unlimited, but other advantages were less obvious.

Satellite Advantages

For example, satellite technology allowed a more flexible choice of frequencies. The coverage of a terrestrial radio navigation system is limited by the propagation characteristics of electromagnetic radiation near the ground. To achieve long ranges, the basically spherical shape of the earth favors low frequencies that stay close to the surface. One system, *Loran-C* (long range navigation-C), can be used to determine positions up to 3000 km from a fixed transmitter, but its frequency must be in the *LF* (low-frequency range) at 100 kHz. *Omega*, another hyperbolic radio navigation system, can be used at ranges of 9000 km, but its 10- to 14-kHz frequency is so low it's actually audible. (The range of human hearing is about 20Hz to 15kHz.) These low frequencies have drawbacks. They can be profoundly affected by unpredictable ionospheric disturbances. And modeling the reduced propagation velocity of a radio signal over land can be difficult. But earth-orbiting satellites could allow the use of a broader range of frequencies, and signals emanating from space are simply more reliable.

Satellites could use high-frequency signals, offer limitless coverage and many other advantages. However, development of the technology for launching transmitters with sophisticated frequency standards into orbit was not accomplished immediately. Therefore, some of the earliest extra-terrestrial positioning was done with optical systems.

Optical Systems

Optical tracking of satellites is a logical extension of astronomy. The astronomic determination of a position on the earth's surface from star observations, certainly the oldest method, is actually very similar to extrapolating the position of a satellite from a photograph of it crossing the night sky. In fact, the astronomical coordinates, *right ascension* α, and *declination* δ, of such a satellite image are calculated from the background fixed stars.

Triangulation with Photographs

Photographic images that combine reflective satellites and fixed stars are taken with *ballistic cameras* whose chopping shutters open and close very fast. The technique causes both the satellites, illuminated by sunlight or earth-based beacons, and the fixed stars to appear on the plate as a series of dots. Comparative analysis of photographs provides data to calculate the orbit of the satellite. Photographs of the same satellite made by cameras thousands of kilometers apart can thus be used to determine the camera's positions by triangulation. The accuracy of such networks has been estimated as high as ± 5 meters.

Laser Ranging

Other optical system are much more accurate. One called *SLR* (satellite laser ranging) is similar to measuring the distance to a satellite using a sophisticated EDM. A laser is aimed from the earth to satellites equipped with retro reflectors, and the elapsed time from transmission to reception yields the range. The same technique, called *LLR* (lunar laser ranging), is used to measure distances to the moon using corner cube reflectors left there during manned missions. These techniques can achieve positions of centimeter precision when information is gathered from several stations. However, one drawback is that the observations must be spread over long periods, up to a month, and they also depend on two-way measurement.

Optical Drawbacks

While some optical methods, like SLR, can achieve extraordinary accuracies regardless of baseline length, they can at the same time be subject to some chronic difficulties. Some methods require skies to be clear simultaneously at widely spaced sites. Even then, local atmospheric turbulence causes the images of the satellites to scintillate. The bulky equipment is expensive and optical refraction is difficult to model. In the case of photographic techniques, emulsions cannot be made completely free from irregularities. So, while optical tracking remains a significant part of the satellite management programs of NASA and other agencies, it has been supplanted by more advanced systems for geodetic positioning.

Extraterrestrial Radio Positioning

Satellite Tracking

The earliest American extraterrestrial systems were designed to assist in satellite tracking and satellite orbit determination, not geodesy. Some of the methods used did not find their way into the GPS technology at all. Some early systems relied on the reflection of signals, transmissions from ground stations that would either bounce off the satellite or stimulate onboard transponders. But systems that required the user to broadcast a signal from the earth to the satellite were not favorably considered in designing the then-new GPS system. Any requirement that the user reveal his position was less attractive to the military planners responsible for developing GPS. They favored a passive system that allowed the user to simply receive the satellite's signal. So, with their two-way measurements and utilization of several frequencies to resolve the cycle ambiguity, many early extraterrestrial tracking systems were harbingers of the modern EDM technology more than GPS.

Prime Minitrack

However, elsewhere there were ranging techniques useful to GPS. NASA's first satellite tracking system, *Prime Minitrack*, relied on phase difference measurements of a single-frequency carrier broadcast by the satellites themselves and received by two separate ground-based antennas. This technique is called *interferometry*. Interferometry is the measurement of the difference between the phases of signals that originate at a common source but travel different paths to the receivers. The combination of such signals, collected by two separate receivers, invariably finds them out of step, since one has traveled a longer distance than the other. Analysis of the signal's phase difference can yield very accurate ranges, and interferometry has become an indispensable measurement technique in several scientific fields.

VLBI

For example, very long baseline interferometry (VLBI) did not originate in the field of satellite tracking or aircraft navigation, but in radio astronomy. The technique was so successful it is still in use today. Radio telescopes, sometimes on different continents, tape-record the microwave

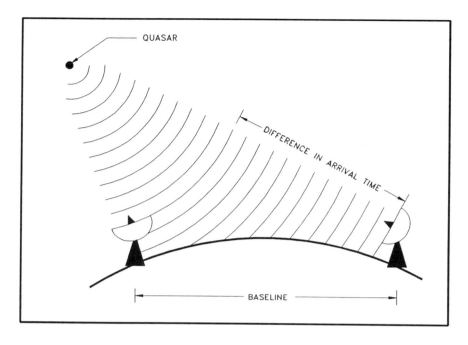

Figure 3.1. Very Long Baseline Interferometry.

signals from quasars, starlike points of light billions of light-years from earth (Figure 3.1).

These recordings are encoded with time tags controlled by hydrogen masers, the most stable of oscillators (clocks). The tapes are then brought together and played back at a central processor. Cross-correlation of the time tags reveals the difference in the instants of a wavefront's arrival at the two telescopes. The discovery of the time offset that maximizes the correlation of the signals recorded by the two telescopes yields the distance and direction between them within a few centimeters, over thousands of kilometers.

VLBI's potential for geodetic measurement was realized as early as 1967. But the concept of high-accuracy baseline determination using phase differencing was really proven in the late '70s. A direct line of development leads from the VLBI work of that era by a group from the Massachusetts Institute of Technology to today's most accurate GPS ranging technique, carrier phase measurement. VLBI, along with other extraterrestrial systems like SLR, also provides valuable information on the earth's gravitational field and rotational axis. Without that data, the high accuracy of the modern coordinate systems that are critical to the success of GPS, like the Conventional Terrestrial

System (CTS) would not be possible. But the foundation for routine satellite-based geodesy actually came even earlier, and from a completely different direction. The first prototype satellite of the immediate precursor of the GPS system was launched in 1961. Its range measurements were based on the Doppler effect, not phase differencing, and the system came to be known as *TRANSIT*.

TRANSIT

The Doppler Shift

Satellite technology and the Doppler effect were combined in the first comprehensive earth-orbiting satellite system dedicated to positioning. By tracking Sputnik in 1957, experimenters at Johns Hopkins University found that the Doppler shift of its signal provided enough information to determine the exact moment of its closest approach to the earth. This discovery led to the creation of the Navy Navigational Satellite System (NNSS) and the subsequent launch of six satellites specifically designed to be used for navigation of military aircraft and ships. This same system, eventually known as TRANSIT, was classified in 1964, declassified in 1967, and has been widely used in civilian surveying ever since (Figure 3.2).

TRANSIT Shortcomings

However, the TRANSIT system has some nagging drawbacks. For example, its primary observable is based on the comparison of the nominally constant frequency generated in the receiver with the Doppler-shifted signal received from one satellite at a time. With a constellation of only six satellites, this strategy can leave the observer waiting up to 90 minutes between satellites, and at least two passes are usually required for acceptable accuracy. With an orbit of only 1100 km above the earth, the TRANSIT satellite's orbits are quite low and are, therefore, unusually susceptible to atmospheric drag and gravitational variations, making the calculation of accurate orbital parameters particularly difficult.

TRANSIT and GPS

Through the decades of the '70s and '80s, both the best and the worst aspects of the TRANSIT system were instructive. Some of the most successful strategies of the TRANSIT system have been incor-

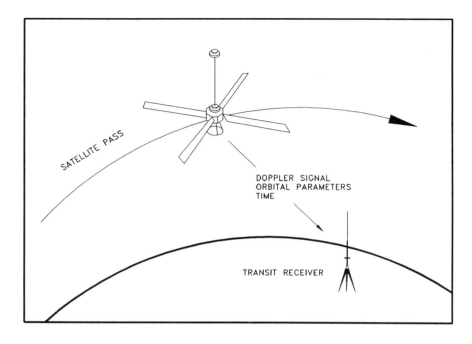

Figure 3.2. Transit Satellite System.

porated into GPS. In both systems, the satellites broadcast their own ephemerides to the receivers. Both systems are divided into three segments: the control segment, including the tracking and upload facilities; the space segment, meaning the satellite themselves; and the user segment, everyone with receivers. In both systems the satellites broadcast two frequencies to allow compensation for the ionospheric dispersion. TRANSIT satellites use the frequencies of 400 MHz and 150 MHz, while GPS uses 1575.42 MHz and 1227.60 MHz. And in both the TRANSIT and GPS systems, each satellite and receiver contains its own frequency standards.

Linking Datums

Perhaps the most significant difference between the TRANSIT system and previous extraterrestrial systems was TRANSIT's capability of linking national and international datums with relative ease. Its facility at strengthening geodetic coordinates laid the groundwork for modern geocentric datums.

NAVSTAR GPS

Orbits and Clocks

In 1973, the early GPS experiments were started. From the beginning of GPS, the plan was to include the best features and improve on the shortcomings of all of the previous work in the field. For example, the GPS satellites have been placed in nearly circular orbits over 20,000 km above the earth, where the consequences of gravity and atmospheric drag are much less severe. And while the low frequency signals of the TRANSIT system make the ionospheric delay very troublesome, the much higher frequency of GPS signals reduce the effect. The rubidium and cesium time clocks in GPS satellites are a marked improvement over the quartz oscillators used in TRANSIT satellites.

Increased Accuracy

TRANSIT's shortcomings restrict the practical accuracy of the system. Submeter work can only be achieved with long occupation on a station (at least a day), augmented by the use of a precise ephemeris for the satellite in postprocessing. GPS provides much more accurate positions in a much shorter time than any of its predecessors, but these improvements are only accomplished by standing on the shoulders of the technologies that have gone before (Table 3.1).

Table 3.1. Technologies Preceding GPS

Name of System	Range	Positional Accuracy in Meters	Features
OMEGA	Worldwide	2,200 CEP	susceptible to VLF propagation anomalies
LORAN-C	U.S. and selected overseas	180 CEP	skywave interference and localized coverage
TRANSIT	Worldwide	submeter in days	long waits between satellite passes
GPS	Worldwide	centimeter in minutes	24 hour worldwide all weather

CEP—circular error probably

Military Application

The genesis of GPS was military. It grew out of the congressional mandate issued to the Departments of Defense and Transportation to consolidate the myriad of navigation systems. Its application to civilian surveying was not part of the original design. In 1973 the DOD directed the Joint Program Office (*JPO*) in Los Angeles to establish the GPS system. Specifically, JPO was asked to create a system with high accuracy and continuous availability in real time that could provide virtually instantaneous positions to both stationary and moving receivers—all features that the TRANSIT system could not supply.

Secure, Passive, and Global

Worldwide coverage and positioning on a common coordinate grid were also required of the new system—a combination that had been difficult, if not impossible, with terrestrial-based systems. It was to be a passive system, which ruled out any transmissions from the users, as had been tried with some previous satellite systems. But the signal was to be secure and resistant to jamming, so codes in the satellite's broadcasts would need to be complex.

Expense and Frequency Allocation

The DOD also wanted the new system to be free from the sort of ambiguity problems that had plagued OMEGA and other radar systems. And DOD did not want the new system to require large expensive equipment, like the optical systems. Finally, frequency allocation was a consideration. The replacement of existing systems would take time, and with so many demands on the available radio spectrum, it was going to be hard to find frequencies for GPS.

Large Capacity Signal

Not only did the specifications for GPS evolve from the experience with earlier positioning systems, so did much of the knowledge needed to satisfy them. Providing 24-hour real-time, high-accuracy navigation for moving vehicles in three dimensions was a tall order. Experience showed part of the answer was a signal that was capable of carrying a very large amount of information efficiently, and that required a large bandwidth. So, the GPS signal was given a double-sided 10-MHZ bandwidth. But that was still not enough, so the idea of simultaneous observation of several satellites was also incorporated into the GPS system to accommodate the requirement. That decision had far-reaching implications.

The Satellite Constellation

Unlike some of its predecessors, GPS needed to have not one, but at least four satellites above an observer's horizon for adequate positioning. Even more, if possible. And the achievement of full-time worldwide GPS coverage would require this condition to be satisfied at all times, anywhere on or near the earth. Toward that end, several orbital arrangements of the satellites were tried. Today, the constellation consists of 24 satellites, four in each of six orbital planes, with each plane inclined to the equator by 55° (Figure 3.3). This design covers the globe completely, and means that multiple satellite coverage is always available.

Spread Spectrum Signal

The specification for the GPS system required all-weather performance and correction for ionospheric propagation delay. TRANSIT had shown that could be accomplished with a dual-frequency transmission from the satellites, but it had also proved that a higher frequency was needed. The GPS signal needed to be secure and resistant to both jamming and multipath. A spread spectrum, meaning spreading the frequency over a band wider than the minimum required for the information it carries, helped on all counts. This wider band also provided ample space for pseudorandom noise encoding, a fairly new development at the time. The PRN codes allowed the GPS receiver to acquire signals from several satellites simultaneously and still distinguish them from one another.

GPS in Civilian Surveying

As mentioned earlier, application to civilian surveying was not part of the original concept of GPS. The civilian use of GPS grew up through partnerships between various public, private, and academic organizations. Nevertheless, while the military was still testing its first receivers, GPS was already in use by civilians. Geodetic surveys were actually underway with commercially available receivers early in the 1980s.

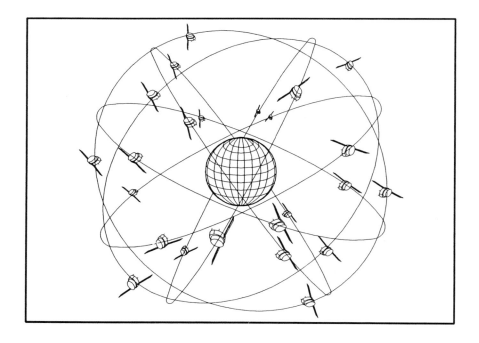

Figure 3.3. Satellite Coverage Constellation.

Federal Specifications

The Federal Radionavigation Plan of 1984, a biennial document including official policies regarding radionavigation, set the predictable and repeatable accuracy of civil and commercial use of GPS at 100 meters horizontally and 156 meters vertically. This specification meant that the C/A code ranging for Standard Positioning Service could be defined by a horizontal circle with a radius of 100 meters, 95 percent of the time. However, that same year civilian users were already achieving results up to six orders of magnitude beyond that limit.

Interferometry

By using interferometry, the technique that had worked so well with Prime Minitrack and VLBI, civilian users were showing that GPS surveying was capable of extraordinary results. In the summer of 1982 a research group at the Massachusetts Institute of Technology (MIT) tested an early GPS receiver and achieved accuracies of 1 and 2 ppm of the station separation. Over a period of several years, extensive testing was conducted around the world that confirmed and improved on these results. In 1984, a GPS network was produced to control the construction of the Stanford Linear Accelerator. This GPS network provided accuracy at the millimeter level. In other words, by using the carrier phase observable instead of code ranging, private firms and researchers were going far beyond the accuracies the U.S. Government expected to be available to civilian users of GPS.

The interferometric solutions made possible by computerized processing developed with earlier extraterrestrial systems were applied to GPS by the first commercial users. The combination made the accuracy of GPS its most impressive characteristic, but it hardly solved every problem. For many years, the system was restricted by the shortage of satellites as the constellation slowly grew. The necessity of having four satellites above the horizon restricted the available observation sessions to a few, sometimes inconvenient, windows of time. Another drawback of GPS for the civilian user was the cost and the limited application of both the hardware and the software. GPS was too expensive and too inconvenient for everyday use.

Civil Applications of GPS

But today, with a mask angle of 10°, there are periods when up to 10 satellites are above the horizon. GPS receivers have grown from only a handful to more than 40 built by a dozen different manufacturers. Some push the envelope to achieve ever-higher accuracy; others offer less sophistication and lower cost. The civilian user's options are broader with GPS than any previous satellite positioning system—so broad that, as originally planned, GPS will likely replace its predecessors in both the military and civilian arenas. In fact, GPS has developed into a system that has more civilian applications and users than military ones. But the extraordinary range of GPS equipment and software requires the user to be familiar with an ever-expanding body of knowledge.

GPS SEGMENT ORGANIZATION

The Space Segment

Though there has been some evolution in the arrangement, today's GPS constellation consists of 24 satellites, four in each of six orbital planes (Figure 3.3). Each orbital plane is inclined to the equator by an angle of 55°, and each of the six is rotated 60° from its neighbor.

Twenty-one of the satellites are operational, and there are three active spares orbiting with them, ready to replace any malfunctioning satellite. The plan also includes seven satellites available for launch as they are needed. Up to three satellites can fail before it will be necessary to launch a replacement.

Orbital Period

NAVSTAR satellites are about 20,000 km above the earth in a *posigrade* orbit. A posigrade orbit is one that moves in the same direction as the earth's rotation. Since each satellite is nearly three times the earth's radius above the surface, its orbital period is 12 sidereal hours.

4 Minute Difference

When an observer actually performs a GPS survey project, one of the most noticeable aspects of a satellite's motion is that it returns to the same position in the sky about 4 minutes earlier each day. This apparent regression is attributable to the difference between 24 solar hours and 24 sidereal hours. GPS satellites actually retrace the same orbital path twice each sidereal day, but since their observers measure time in solar units the orbits do not look quite so regular to them. The satellites lose 4 minutes with each successive solar day. For example, if the satellites are in a particularly favorable configuration for measurement and the observer wishes to take advantage of the same arrangement the following day, he or she would be well advised to remember the same configuration will occur 4 minutes earlier on the solar time scale. Both Universal Time (UT) and GPS time are measured in solar, not sidereal units. It is possible that the satellites will be pushed 50 km higher in the future to remove their current 4-minute regression, but for now it remains.

Design

The GPS constellation was designed to satisfy several critical concerns. Among them were the best possible coverage of the earth with the fewest number of satellites, the reduction of the effects of gravitational and atmospheric drag, sufficient upload and monitoring capability with all control stations located on American soil, and, finally, the achievement of maximum accuracy.

DOP

The distribution of the satellites above an observer's horizon has a direct bearing on the quality of the position derived from them. Like some of its forerunners, the accuracy of a GPS position is subject to a geometric phenomenon called *dilution of precision (DOP)*. This number is somewhat similar to the strength of figure consideration in the design of a triangulation network. DOP concerns the geometric strength of the figure described by the positions of the satellites with respect to one another (Figure 3.4).

Four or more satellites must be above the observer's mask angle for the simultaneous solution of the clock offset and three dimensions of the receiver's position. But if all of those satellites are crowded together in one part of the sky, the position would be likely to have an unacceptable uncertainty. That uncertainty can be represented by a number called the *geometric dilution of precision (GDOP)*. GDOP represents the uncertainty that may be expected in the three position coordinates and the clock offset from a particular configuration of satellites. And when the GDOP is high, accuracy suffers.

GDOP

The larger the volume of the body defined by the lines from the receiver to the satellites, the better the satellite geometry and the lower the GDOP (Figure 3.5). An ideal arrangement of four satellites would be one directly above the receiver, the others 120° from one another in azimuth near the horizon. With that distribution the GDOP would be nearly 1, the lowest possible value. In practice, the lowest GDOPs are generally around 2. For example, if the standard deviation of a position, its UERE, were ± 5 meters and the GDOP 2, then the actual uncertainty of the position would be 2 times ± 5 meters or ± 10 meters. In static applications the configuration of the satellites over the entire span of the observation is an important consideration. As the satellites move, the GDOP changes, and may effect the length of the observation session necessary to achieve a desired accuracy.

Other DOP

There are other DOP factors used to evaluate the uncertainties in the components of a receiver's position. For example, there is horizontal dilution of precision *(HDOP)* and vertical dilution of precision *(VDOP)*, where the uncertainty of a solution for positioning has been isolated into its hori-

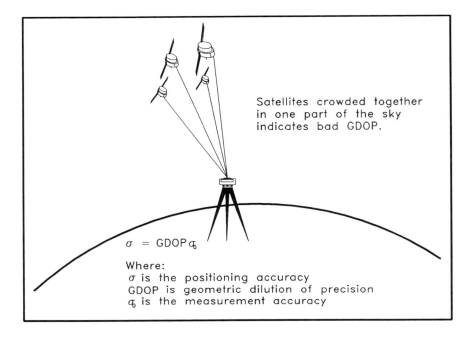

Satellites crowded together in one part of the sky indicates bad GDOP.

$$\sigma = GDOP\, \sigma_0$$

Where:
σ is the positioning accuracy
GDOP is geometric dilution of precision
σ_0 is the measurement accuracy

Figure 3.4. Dilution of Precision.

zontal and vertical components, respectively. When both horizontal and vertical components are combined, the uncertainty is called *PDOP*, position dilution of precision. There is also *TDOP*, time dilution of precision, that indicates only the clock offset; and *RDOP*, relative dilution of precision, that includes the number of receivers, the number of satellites they can handle, the length of the observing session as well as the geometry of the satellite's configuration.

Outages

When a DOP factor exceeds a maximum limit in a particular location, indicating an unacceptable level of uncertainty exists over a period of time, that period is known as an *outage*. This expression of uncertainty is useful both in interpreting measured baselines and planning a GPS survey.

Satellite Positions in Mission Planning

The position of the satellites above an observer's horizon is a critical consideration in planning a GPS survey. So, most software packages pro-

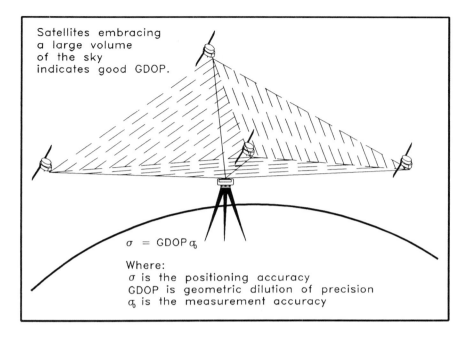

Figure 3.5. Geometric Dilution of Precision.

vide various methods of illustrating the satellite configuration for a particular location over a specified period of time. A commonly used plot of the satellite's tracks is constructed on a graphical representation of the half of the celestial sphere. The observer's zenith is shown in the center and the horizon on the perimeter. The program usually draws arcs by connecting the points of the instantaneous azimuths and elevations of the satellites above a specified mask angle. These arcs then represent the paths of the available satellites over the period of time and the place specified by the user.

In Figure 3.6, the plot of the polar coordinates of the available satellites with respect to time and position is just one of several tables and graphs available to help the GPS user visualize the constellation. The variety of the tools to help the observer predict satellite visibility underlines the importance of their configuration to successful positioning.

Satellite Names

The first GPS satellite was launched February 22, 1978 and is known as *Navstar 1*. An unfortunate complication is that this satellite is also known

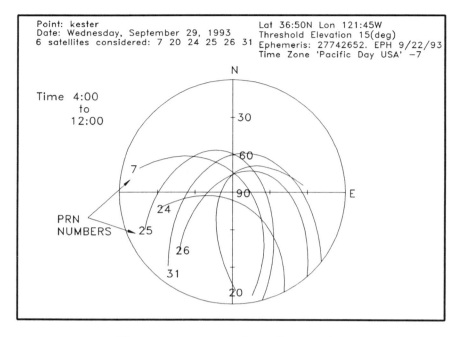

Point: kester
Date: Wednesday, September 29, 1993
6 satellites considered: 7 20 24 25 26 31

Lat 36:50N Lon 121:45W
Threshold Elevation 15(deg)
Ephemeris: 27742652. EPH 9/22/93
Time Zone 'Pacific Day USA' −7

Figure 3.6. Projected Satellite Tracks.

as PRN 4, just as Navstar 2 is known as PRN 7. The Navstar number is the order of launch and the PRN number refers to the weekly segment of the P code that has been assigned to the satellite, and there are still more identifiers. Each GPS satellite has an Inter Range Operation Number, a NASA catalog number, and an orbital position number as well. However, in most literature, and to the GPS receivers themselves, the PRN number is the most important.

The 11 GPS satellites launched from Vandenberg Air Force Base between 1978 and 1985 are known as *Block I satellites*. The designation includes all of the prototype satellites built to validate the concept of GPS positioning. This test constellation of Block I satellites was inclined by 63° to the equator instead of the current specification of 55°. They can be maneuvered by hydrazine thrusters operated by the control stations.

Block I

The Block I satellites weigh 845 kg in final orbit. They are powered by three rechargeable nickel-cadmium batteries and 7.25 square meters of single-degree solar panels. These experimental satellites have served to

point the way for some of the improvements found in subsequent generations. For example, even with the backup systems of two rubidium and
two cesium oscillators onboard each satellite, the clocks have proved to be
the weakest components. The satellites themselves can only store sufficient information for 3½ days of independent operation. And the uploads
from the control segment are not secure; they are not encrypted. Still, all
11 achieved orbit, except Navstar 7, and it is remarkable that 5 of them are
still operational, despite a design life of only 4½ years.

Block II

The next generation of GPS satellites are known as *Block II satellites*. There will be 28 of them built. The first left Cape Canaveral on
February 14, 1989, almost 14 years after the first GPS satellite was launched.
It was about twice as heavy as the first Block I satellite and is expected to
have a design life of 7½ years. The Block II satellites can operate up to 14
days without an upload from the control segment and their uploads are
encrypted. The satellites themselves are radiation hardened, and their signals are subject to selective availability. The launch schedule of the Block
II satellites has been proceeding smoothly, and every indication is that it
will continue to do so.

Block IIR

The third generation of GPS satellites is known as *Block IIR satellites*; the R stands for *replenishment*. Two significant advancements are
expected from these satellites. First, instead of the cesium and rubidium
clocks of the previous generations, these satellites will use hydrogen masers. Hydrogen masers are much more stable than earlier oscillators. Second, the Block IIR satellites will have enhanced autonomous navigation
capability because of their use of intersatellite linkage. These GPS satellites will not only be capable of self-navigation, they will also provide other
spacecraft equipped with an onboard GPS receiver with the data they
need to define their own positions.

Signal Deterioration

While the signals from Block I satellites are not subject to any officially sanctioned deterioration, the same cannot be said of the Block II
satellites (Figure 3.7). In the interest of national security, the signals from

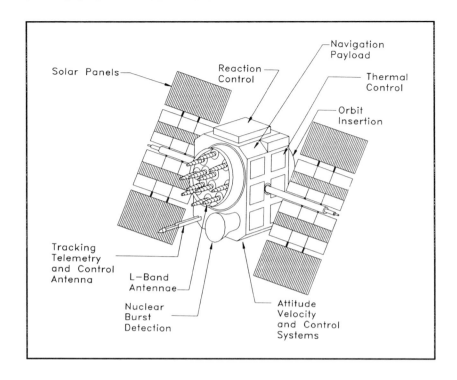

Figure 3.7. GPS Block II Satellite.

the operational constellation of GPS satellites, including the Block II and IIR satellites, have been and will be intentionally degraded periodically. The selective availability (SA) of the C/A code has been implemented by disrupting the satellite clock frequency from time to time since April 1990. The P code will also be intermittently supplanted by the encrypted Y code in a procedure known as *antispoofing (AS)*. However, neither of these procedures significantly affect relative positioning methods that rely on the carrier beat phase observable.

GPS Satellites

All GPS satellites have some common characteristics. They all have three-dimensional stabilization to ensure that their solar arrays are perpendicular to the sun and their antennae are pointed at the earth. Even so, the satellites must pass through the shadow of the earth from time to time. During an eclipse, the absence of the pressure of solar radiation is over in less than an hour, but it must be taken into account. Onboard batteries provide power, but of more concern is the prediction of precise ephemeris information at such times. In a related issue, all satellites are equipped with thermostatically controlled heaters and reflective insulation to maintain the optimum temperature for the oscillator's operation.

THE CONTROL SEGMENT

As mentioned in Chapter 1, there are several government tracking and uploading facilities distributed around the world. Taken together, these facilities are known as the *Control Segment*.

MCS

The Master Control Station (MCS), once located at Vandenberg Air Force Base in California now resides at the Consolidated Space Operations Center (CSOC) at Falcon Air Force Base in Colorado Springs, Colorado. This station computes updates for the Navigation message, including the broadcast ephemeris and satellite clock corrections derived from about 1 week of the tracking information it collects from five monitoring stations around the world. By utilizing the five additional monitoring stations under the jurisdiction of the Defense Mapping Agency, an official postcomputed precise ephemeris is available to the GPS user. Unfortunately, it takes two weeks for this postcomputed ephemeris to find its way to users. The MCS also initiates satellite repositioning and replacement as they become necessary.

Other Stations

The monitoring stations located at Ascension Island, Colorado Springs, Diego Garcia, Hawaii, and Kwajalein are each equipped with a dual-frequency GPS receiver and a cesium clock. They observe P code pseudoranges and integrated Doppler measurements from all available satellites. Their measurement of the satellite's actual position is then compared with the latest reference ephemeris to discover the misclosures between the two. And the ranges are then smoothed by a *Kalman filter* to create the new estimates of the satellite's position and speed.

Kalman Filtering

Kalman filtering, named for R.E. Kalman's recursive solution for least-squares filtering (Kalman, 1960), has been applied to the results of radionavigation for several decades. It is a statistical method of smoothing and condensing large amounts of data. One of its uses in GPS is reduction of the pseudoranges measured at 1.5-second intervals between a monitoring station and a satellite. Kalman filtering is used to a condense them into a smoothed set of pseudoranges for a 15-minute period. The results are transmitted to the Master Control Station, where their processing involves still more filtering.

An Analogy

Kalman filtering can be illustrated by the example of an automobile speedometer. Imagine the needle of an automobile's speedometer has a bent cable and is fluctuating between 64 and 72 mph as the car moves down the road. The driver might estimate the actual speed at 68 mph. Although not accepting the speedometers measurements literally, he has taken them into consideration and constructed an internal model of his velocity. If the driver further depresses the accelerator and the needle responds by moving up, his reliance on the speedometer increases. Despite its vacillation, the needle has reacted as the driver thought it should. It went higher as the car accelerated. This behavior illustrates a predictable correlation between one variable, acceleration, and another, speed. Now he is more confident in his ability to predict the behavior of the speedometer. The driver is illustrating *adaptive gain*, meaning that he is fine-tuning his model as he receives new information about the measurements. As he does, a truer picture of the relationship between the readings from the speedometer and his actual speed emerges, without recording every single number as the needle jumps around. The driver in this analogy is like the Kalman filter.

Without this ability to take the huge amounts of satellite data and condense them into a manageable number of components, GPS processors would be overwhelmed. Kalman filtering is used in the uploading process to reduce the data to the satellite clock offset and drift, 6 orbital parameters, 3 solar radiation pressure parameters, biases of the monitoring station's clock, a model of the tropospheric effect, and earth rotational components.

Constant Tracking

Every GPS satellite is being tracked by at least one of the control segment's monitoring stations at all times. The MCS sends its updates around the world to four strategically located uploading stations. They in turn transmit the new Navigation messages to each satellite. The Block II satellites can function without new uploads for 14 days and Block I satellites for only 3½ days. In any event, the older their Navigation message gets, the more the accuracy of their positioning service deteriorates.

Postcomputed Ephemerides

This system is augmented by several other tracking networks that produce postcomputed ephemerides. Their impetus have been several: the necessity of timely orbital information with more precision than the broadcast ephemeris, the correlation of the terrestrial coordinate systems with the orbital system through VLBI and SLR sites, independence from the DOD, and profit. Some examples of global tracking networks are, the Cooperative International GPS Network *(CIGNET)* and the International GPS Geodynamics Service *(IGS)*. There are also many regional facilities such as the private tracking network operated by the manufacturer of the Macrometer™ since 1983, and the Australian GPS pilot project for orbit determination.

CIGNET is managed by the National Geodetic Survey *(NGS)*, and incorporates information from nearly two dozen tracking facilities around the world. Located at VLBI sites, some of the facilities can provide their data to NGS nightly, which, after processing, makes the data available to users the following day in both ASCII and binary files. The quick access of the CIGNET tracking data and the fact that its facilities record both carrier phase as well as P code ranges are important departures from the official control segment procedures.

The User Segment

The military plans to build a GPS receiver into virtually all of its ships, aircraft, and terrestrial vehicles. In fact, the Block IIR satellites may be harbingers of the incorporation of more and more receivers into extraterrestrial vehicles as well. But even with such widespread use in the military, civilian GPS will be still more extensive.

Constantly Increasing Application of GPS

The uses the general public finds for GPS will undoubtedly continue to grow as the cost and size of the receivers continues to shrink. The number of users in surveying will be small when compared with the large numbers of trains, cars, boats, and airplanes with GPS receivers. GPS will be used to position all categories of civilian transportation, as well as law enforcement and emergency vehicles. Nevertheless, surveying and geodesy have the distinction of being the first practical application of GPS, and the most sophisticated uses and users are still under its purview. That situation will likely continue for some time.

Next Chapter

The number, range, and complexity of GPS receivers available to surveyors has exploded in recent years. There are widely varying prices and features that sometimes make it difficult to match the equipment with the application. Chapter 4 will be devoted to a detailed discussion of the GPS receivers themselves.

REFERENCES

Kalman, R.E. "A New Approach to Linear Filtering and Prediction Problems," Trans. of the ASME *Journal of Basic Engineering,* (1960), pp. 35–45.

Chapter Four

Receivers and Methods

COMMON FEATURES OF GPS RECEIVERS

Receivers for GPS Surveying

Probably the most important hardware in a GPS surveying operation are the receivers (Figure 4.1). Their characteristics and capabilities influence the techniques available to the user throughout the work, from the initial planning to the postmission processing. There are literally hundreds of GPS receivers on the market, and while only a portion of that number are appropriate for GPS surveying, all share the same fundamental elements.

The Antenna

The antenna collects the satellite's signals. Its main function is the conversion of electromagnetic waves into electric currents sensible to the radio receiver. Several antenna designs are possible in GPS, but the satellite's signals have such low power densities that antenna efficiency is critical. About a third of the receivers have an antenna built in, but nearly all can accommodate a separate tripod-mounted antenna as well. These separate antennas with their connecting coaxial cables in standard

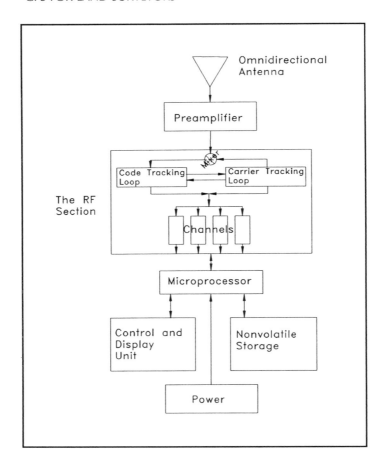

Figure 4.1. A Block Diagram of a Code Correlation Receiver.

lengths from 10 to 60 meters are usually available from the receiver manufacturer.

Approximately three-quarters of the receiver manufacturers offer a *microstrip* antenna. The microstrip can receive one or both GPS frequencies. It is durable and compact and has a simple construction. The next most commonly used antenna is a single frequency configuration known as a *dipole*. The least common design is the *helix* antenna. Like the microstrip, the helix can receive both L1 and L2, but while the microstrip is virtually flat, the helix usually has a high profile. Still, the pattern of its effective area, that is, its *gain pattern*, offers some advantages.

Nearly Hemispheric Coverage

The gain pattern of a GPS antenna should provide a nearly full hemisphere of coverage, eliminating any need to aim it at the source of the signal. But the coverage is not usually an absolute hemisphere, partly because most surveying applications filter the signals from very low elevations to reduce the effects of multipath and atmospheric delays. Also, the contours of equal phase around the antenna's electronic center, that is, the *phase center*, are not themselves perfectly spherical.

Antenna Orientation

In an ideal GPS antenna, the phase center of the gain pattern would be exactly coincident with its actual center. If such perfection were possible, the physical centering of the antenna over a point on the earth would ensure its electronic centering as well, but that absolute certainty remains elusive for several reasons. For example, the location of the phase center changes slightly with the satellite's signal. It is different for the L2 signal than it is for the L1 signal. In addition, as the azimuth, intensity, and elevation of the received signal change, the difference between the phase center and the physical center can move as much as a couple of centimeters.

Fortunately, these variations are systematic. To compensate for some of this offset error, about half of the receiver manufacturers recommend that users take care, when making simultaneous observations on a network of points, that their antennas are all oriented in the same direction. Several manufacturers even provide reference marks on the antenna so that each one may be rotated to the same azimuth; that way, they are expected to maintain the same relative position between their physical and electronic centers when subsequent observations are made.

Height of Instrument

The antenna's configuration also affects another measurement critical to successful GPS surveying—the height of instrument. The measurement of the height of the instrument in a GPS survey is normally made to some reference mark on the antenna. However, it must often include an added correction to bring the total vertical distance to the antenna's phase center.

The RF Section

Channels

After the satellite's signals are collected by the antenna they are preamplified and passed to the core of the GPS receiver, the radio frequency *(RF)* section. The antenna itself does not sort the information it gathers. The signals from several satellites enter the receiver simultaneously. But in the *channels* of the RF section the undifferentiated signals are identified and segregated from one another.

A channel in a GPS receiver is not unlike a channel in a television set. It is hardware, or a combination of hardware and (computer) software, designed to separate one signal from all the others. Again, just as with a television, a GPS receiver can accommodate broadcasts of several frequencies by assigning those frequencies to individual channels within the receiver. But at any given moment, only one frequency from one satellite can be on one channel at a time. A receiver may have as few as 3 or as many as 40 physical channels. Twelve channels is typical.

Multiplexing

A receiver with a 12-channel configuration is entirely adequate for tracking all the satellites above the observer's horizon, but on only one frequency; L1, for example. But there are other ways to arrange the tracking for the same 12-channel receiver. For example, it can be designed to receive two frequencies, both L1 and L2, but then it can only track six satellites. The limiting factor is that each channel must be dedicated to only one signal at a time. However, there is still another technique, known as *multiplexing* or *sequencing*. This technique increases tracking capability by switching from one signal to another very quickly.

When a GPS receiver's channels are not continuously dedicated to just one satellite's signal or one frequency, it is called a *multiplexing* or a *sequencing* receiver. While a *multiplexing* receiver must still dedicate one frequency from one satellite to one channel at a time, it makes that time very short. For example, one channel may be used to track the signal from one satellite for only 20 milliseconds, leave that signal and track another for 20 milliseconds, and then return to the first, or even move on to a third.

This strategy of switching channels is used less today than it was formerly. There are three reasons. Continuous tracking receivers with dedicated channels are faster; they have a more certain phase lock, and they possess a superior signal-to-noise ratio *(SNR)*.

Tracking Methods

Whether continuous or switching channels are used, a receiver must be able to discriminate between the incoming signals. They may be differentiated by their unique C/A codes on L1, their Doppler shifts, or some other method, but in the end each signal is assigned to its own channel. Then several tracking methods are possible; among them are: *code correlation*, *code phase,* or *signal squaring*.

Code-Correlation

The code-correlation technique is unique among the three. While code phase and signal squaring might both be called *codeless techniques*, code-correlation receivers can use every part of the satellite's signal: all the information in the Navigation message, the unmodulated carrier wave, and the PRN codes. Receivers of this type require specific knowledge of the PRN codes for the initial stage of their processing, but few use both the C/A code and the P code; most rely solely on the C/A code. The Control Segments encryption of the P code into the more secure Y-codes, a procedure known as *antispoofing* (AS) has discouraged manufacturers from depending on the more precise code.

Pseudoranging

Today, most receivers use code-correlation, and their first procedure in processing an incoming satellite signal is synchronization of the C/A code from the satellite's L1 broadcast, with a replica C/A code generated by the receiver itself. The details of this process are more fully described in Chapter 1. But for the purpose of this discussion, recall that when there is no initial match between the satellite's code and the receiver's replica, the receiver time shifts, or *slews*, the code it is generating until the optimum correlation is found. Then a code tracking loop, the delay lock loop, keeps them aligned. The time shift discovered in that process is a measure of the signal's travel time from the satellite to the phase center of the receiver's antenna. Multiplying this time delay by the speed of light gives a range. But it is called a *pseudorange* in recognition of the fact that it is contaminated by the errors and biases set out in Chapter 2.

Carrier Phase Measurement

This process not only provides the receiver with a pseudorange to the satellite, but access to the Navigation message as well. It can read the ephemeris and the almanac information, use GPS time, and, for those receivers that do utilize the P code, use the hand-over word on every subframe as a stepping stone to tracking the more precise code. But while most receivers do not track the P code, neither is the precision of a C/A code pseudorange alone adequate for the majority of surveying applications. Therefore, the next step in signal processing for most code correlation receivers involves the carrier phase observable.

Just as it produces a replica of the incoming code, a correlation receiver also produces a replica of the incoming carrier wave. In this case, the foundation of carrier phase measurement is the combination these two frequencies. Remember, the incoming signal from the satellite is subject to an ever-changing Doppler shift, while the replica within the receiver is nominally constant.

Carrier Tracking Loop

The process begins after the PRN code has done its job and the code tracking loop is locked. Then, by mixing the satellite's signal with the replica carrier, the receiver eliminates all the phase modulations, strips the codes from the incoming carrier, and simultaneously creates two intermediate or beat frequencies. One is the sum of the combined frequencies, and the other is the difference. The receiver selects the latter, the difference, with a device known as a *bandpass filter*. Then this signal is sent on to the *carrier tracking loop,* where the voltage-controlled oscillator is continuously adjusted to follow the beat frequency exactly.

Doppler Shift

As the satellite passes overhead, the range between the receiver and the satellite changes. That steady change is reflected in a smooth and continuous movement of the phase of the signal coming into the receiver. The rate of that change is reflected in the constant variation of the signal's Doppler shift. But if the receiver's oscillator frequency is matching these variations exactly, as they are happening, it will duplicate the incoming signal's Doppler shift and phase. This strategy makes measurement of the carrier beat phase observable, a matter of simply counting the elapsed cycles and adding the fractional phase of the receiver's own oscillator. Some of the details of the process are more fully described in Chapter 1. But for the purpose of this discussion, recall that the measurement of the difference between the phase of the incoming Doppler-shifted carrier wave and the phase of the reference carrier generated by the receiver at preset epochs can provide a range with an accuracy of a couple of millimeters. Therefore, the addition of the carrier beat phase observable allows the code correlation receiver to achieve much higher accuracy than it could accomplish with a pseudorange alone.

Signal Squaring

Another method of codeless tracking is called *signal squaring*. It was first used in the earliest civilian GPS receivers, supplanting proposals for a TRANSIT-like Doppler solution. It does not use the codes carried by the satellite's signal. It makes no use of pseudoranging and relies exclusively on the carrier phase observable. Like other methods, it depends on the creation of an intermediate or beat frequency. But with signal squaring, the beat frequency is created by multiplying the incoming carrier by itself. The result has double the frequency and half the wavelength of the original. It is squared.

There are some drawbacks to the method. For example, in the process of squaring the carrier, it is stripped of all its codes. The chips of the P code, the C/A code, and the Navigation message, normally impressed onto the carrier by 180° phase shifts are eliminated entirely. As discussed in Chapter 1, the signals broadcast by the satellites have phase shifts called *code states* that change from +1 to −1 and vice versa, but squaring the carrier converts them all to exactly 1. The result is that the codes themselves are wiped out. Therefore, this method must acquire information such as almanac data and clock corrections from other sources. Other drawbacks of squaring the carrier include the deterioration of the signal-to-noise ratio because when the carrier is squared the background noise is squared too, and cycle slips occur at twice the original carrier frequency.

But signal squaring has its upside as well. It reduces susceptibility to multipath. It has no dependence on PRN codes and is not hindered by the encryption of the P code. The technique works as well on L2 as it does on L1, and that facilitates dual-frequency ionospheric delay correction. Therefore, signal squaring can provide high accuracy over long baselines.

Codeless Pseudoranging

Another technique that was also used in early GPS receivers is known as *code phase*. Like signal squaring, it does not use codes and is sometimes known as *codeless pseudoranging*. It relies on the codes' chipping rates rather than the codes themselves. The received carrier, L1 or L2, is compressed to a slower frequency before being multiplied by itself. However, in this case the multiplier is a delayed version of the received signal, offset by half of the received PRN codes' chipping rate, either the C/A or P code. This limits the technique to a lower accuracy than the carrier beat phase observable, since the units of its measurement must be the wavelengths of the codes; that is, about 293 meters for the C/A code and 29.3 meters for the P code. And like other codeless methods it cannot provide access to the Navigation message's almanac and clock offset information.

Most Receivers Combine Measurement Methods

The RF section and microprocessor of most civilian GPS receivers are capable of combining measurements in various ways. More than half provide their users with the pseudorange, carrier phase, code phase, and integrated Doppler observations. About a quarter of them do not provide the most accurate, the carrier phase observable, and a few do not measure the code pseudoranges. But nearly all GPS receivers measure Doppler data, even though it is not always included in their output.

Range Rate

Doppler information has broad application in signal processing. It can be used to discriminate between the signals from various GPS satellites, to determine integer ambiguities in kinematic surveying (more about that later), as a help in the detection of cycle slips, and as an additional independent observable for point positioning. But perhaps the most important application of Doppler data is the determination of the *range rate* between a receiver and a satellite (Figure 4.2). Range rate is a term used to mean the rate at which the range between a satellite and a receiver changes over a particular period of time.

With respect to the receiver, the satellite is always in motion, of course, even if the receiver is static. But the receiver may be in motion as well, as it is in kinematic GPS. The ability to determine the instantaneous velocity of a moving vehicle has always been a primary application of GPS and is based on the fact that the Doppler-shift frequency of a satellite's signal is nearly proportional to its range rate.

The Typical Change in the Doppler Shift

To see how it works, let's look at a *static*, that is, stationary, GPS receiver. The signal received would have its maximum Doppler shift, 4.5

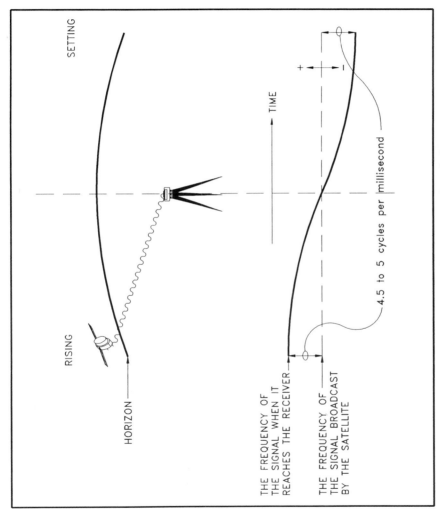

Figure 4.2. Typical GPS Doppler Shift.

to 5 cycles per millisecond, when the satellite is at its maximum range, just as it is rising or setting. But the Doppler shift continuously changes throughout the overhead pass. Immediately after the satellite rises, relative to a particular receiver, its Doppler shift gets smaller and smaller, until the satellite reaches its closest approach. At the instant its radial velocity with respect to the receiver is zero, the Doppler shift of the signal is zero as well. But as the satellite recedes it grows again, negatively, until the Doppler shift once again reaches its maximum extent just as the satellite sets.

Continuously Integrated Doppler

The Doppler-shift and the carrier phase are measured by first combining the received frequencies with the nominally constant reference frequency created by the receiver's oscillator. The difference between the two is a *beat frequency*. The number of beats over a given time interval is known as the *Doppler count* for that interval. Since the beats can be counted much more precisely than their continuously changing frequency can be measured, most GPS receivers just keep track of the accumulated cycles, the Doppler count. The sum of consecutive Doppler counts from an entire satellite pass is often stored, and the data can then be treated like a sequential series of biased range differences. *Continuously integrated Doppler* is such a process. The rate of the change in the continuously integrated Doppler shift of the incoming signal is the same as that of the reconstructed carrier phase.

The Microprocessor

The microprocessor controls the entire receiver, managing its collection of data. The GPS receivers used in surveying usually send these data to the storage unit. For many surveying applications. GPS receivers are not normally expected to produce their final positions instantaneously; that is, in *real time*. But other disciplines routinely rely on such immediate results.

Real-Time Positioning

For example, in some navigation applications of GPS the receiver's microprocessor is expected to provide real-time single-point positioning using unsmoothed code pseudoranges. Such a solution is known as *point positioning*, or *absolute positioning*. Using the C/A code, their results are not accurate by surveying standards, but can be improved by *differential positioning*.

Differential Positioning

Differential positioning still depends on code pseudorange observations, but it requires using two receivers. One receiver is placed on a control station and another on an unknown position. They simultaneously track the same codes from the same satellites, and because many of the errors in the observations are common to both receivers, they tend to cancel each other to some degree.

Differential positioning using a data link between receivers can also provide results in real-time. Some recent improvements in this technology may eventually refine the technique's accuracy markedly, but at present the positions are not nearly as reliable as those achieved with the carrier phase observable. For example, SA's distortion of the satellite clock does not affect postprocessed GPS surveying methods, but it reduces single C/A receiver point positioning to an accuracy of ± 100 meters. While the results can be improved with the differential positioning strategy to ±5 meters, they are still subject to errors and biases from clock behavior, atmosphere, and noise.

Positional Accuracies

Currently, some manufacturers claim submeter positioning for their C/A code pseudorange receivers, but even so, the carrier phase observable can consistently provide a user with centimeter-level, even millimeter-level accuracies. Considering the pace of GPS development, the situation may soon change, but for the moment, the application of convenient handheld receivers offering real-time positioning with C/A code pseudoranges alone is most suitable where relatively low accuracy can be tolerated.

With some Geographical Information Systems (GIS), corner search and mapping work excepted, most GPS surveying requires a higher standard of accuracy. Therefore, the typical solutions are not in real time. In other words, GPS surveying usually employs several *static*, meaning stationary, receivers that simultaneously collect and store data from the same satellites for a period of time known as a *session*. After all the sessions for a day are completed, their data are usually downloaded in a general binary format to the hard disk of a PC for postprocessing. However, not *all* high-accuracy GPS surveying is handled this way. For example, real-time data transfer of carrier phase observations has recently provided good results on short baselines. And some very promising work continues to develop other methods such as kinematic surveying, where the trajectory of a moving GPS receiver is considered; more about that later.

The CDU

GPS receiver's keyboards come in many shapes and sizes, and their displays vary from liquid crystal to video. But every GPS control and display unit *(CDU)* has the same fundamental purpose. They are all designed to provide interactive communication between the user and the receiver's microprocessor.

Typical Displays

The information available from the CDU varies from receiver to receiver. But when four or more satellites are available they generally display the PRN numbers of the satellites being tracked, the receiver's position in three dimensions, and velocity information. Nearly all of them also display the dilution of precision and GPS Time.

The Storage

Most GPS receivers today have internal data logging. A few rely on cassettes or memory cards, but well over half still use disk storage.

Downloading

A large number of range measurements and other pertinent data are sent to the receiver's storage during observation sessions. These data are subsequently downloaded through a serial port to a PC or laptop computer for postprocessing.

The Power

Battery Power

Most receivers operate on battery power over a range from 9 to 36 volts DC. About half of the available carrier phase receivers have an internal power supply, and most will operate 5½ hours or longer on a fully charged 6-amp-hour battery. Most code-tracking receivers, those that do not also use the carrier phase observable, could operate for about 15 hours on the same size battery. A few receivers use AC power or include an AC to DC converter.

CHOOSING A GPS RECEIVER

Receiver Productivity

Choosing the right instrument for a particular application is not easy. Receivers are generally categorized by their physical characteristics, the elements of the GPS signal they can use with advantage, and by the claims about their accuracy. But the effect of these features on a receiver's actual productivity are not always obvious. For example, it is true that the more aspects of the GPS signal a receiver can employ, the greater its flexibility, but so, too, the greater its cost. And separating the capabilities a user needs to do a particular job from those that are really unnecessary is more complicated than simply listing tracking characteristics, storage capacity, power consumption, and other physical statistics. The user must first have some information about how these features relate to a receiver's performance in particular GPS surveying methods.

Typical Concerns

A surveyor generally wants to be able to answer questions like the following. Can this receiver give me the accuracy I need for this particular work? What is the likely rate of productivity on a project like this? What is the actual cost per point? This section is intended to provide some of the information needed to answer such questions. It offers some general guidelines that are useful in choosing a GPS receiver.

Trends in Receiver Development

In the early years of GPS the military concentrated on testing Navigation receivers. But civilians got involved much sooner than expected and took a different direction: receivers with geodetic accuracy.

High Accuracy Early

The first GPS receivers in commercial use were single frequency, six channel, codeless instruments. Their measurements were based on interferometry. As early as the 1980s, those receivers could measure short baselines to millimeter accuracy and long baselines to 1 ppm. It is true the equipment was cumbersome, expensive and, without access to the Navigation message, dependent on external sources for clock and ephemeris information. But they were the first at work in the field and their accuracy was impressive.

Another Direction

During the same era, a parallel trend was underway. The idea was to develop a more portable, dual-frequency, four-channel receiver that could use the Navigation message. Such an instrument did not need external sources for clock and ephemeris information, and could be more self-contained.

More Convenience

Unlike the original codeless receivers that required all units on a survey brought together and their clocks synchronized twice a day, these receivers could operate independently. And while the codeless receivers needed to have satellite ephemeris information downloaded before their observations could begin, this receiver could derive its ephemeris directly from the satellite's signal. Despite these advantages, the instruments developed on this model still weighed more than 40 pounds, cost well over $100,000, and were dependent on P code tracking.

Multichannel and Code-Correlating

A few years later a different kind of multichannel receiver appeared. Instead of the P code, it tracked the C/A code. Instead of using both the L1 and L2 frequencies, it depended on L1 alone, and on that single frequency, it tracked the C/A code and also measured the carrier phase observable. This type of receiver established the basic design for the majority of the GPS receivers surveyors use today. Nearly three-quarters of the civilian GPS receivers now being manufactured for surveying applications use this same strategy. They are multichannel code-correlation receivers. They can recover all of the components of the L1 signal. The C/A code is used to establish the signal lock and initialize the tracking loop. Then the receiver not only reconstructs the carrier wave, it also extracts the satellite clock correction, ephemeris, and other information from the Navigation message. Such receivers are capable of measuring pseudoranges, along with the carrier phase and integrated Doppler observables. Their cost varies from about $10,000 to $40,000, but the average is around $18,000.

Dual-Frequency

Still, as some of the earlier instruments illustrated, the dual-frequency approach does offer significant advantages. It can be used to limit the effects of ionospheric delay, it can increase the reliability of the results over long baselines, and it certainly increases the scope of GPS procedures available to a surveyor. For these reasons, a substantial number of receivers utilize both frequencies.

Receiver manufacturers are currently using several configurations in building dual-frequency receivers. In order to get both carriers without knowledge of the P code, some use a combination of C/A code-correlation and codeless methods. These receivers use code correlation on L1 and then, borrowing an idea from the first GPS receivers, they add signal squaring on L2. The average cost of a GPS receiver with C/A code-correlation on L1 and codeless technology on L2 is around $25,000.

Adding Codeless Capability

By adding codeless technology on the second frequency, such receivers can avail themselves of the advantages of a dual-frequency capability while avoiding the disadvantages of depending on the P code. High on the disadvantage list is anti-spoofing *(AS)*.

Anti-spoofing, or AS, is the encryption of the P code on both L1 and L2. These encrypted codes are known as the Y codes, Y1 and Y2, respectively. When AS is activated, only receivers equipped with an Auxiliary Output Chip *(AOC)* will be able to track the P code. In this way, AS implementation makes civilian access to the precise code very difficult.

Adding P Code Tracking

Nevertheless, with dual-frequency receivers fast becoming the standard for geodetic applications of GPS, a few receivers do track the P code. But just as the idea of an entirely codeless receiver is not used in GPS surveying today, there are no civilian receivers that rely solely on the P code, either. Nearly all receivers that track the P code use the C/A code on L1. Some use both the C/A code and P code tracking on L1, with codeless technology on L2. Some track the P code only when it is not encrypted, and become codeless on L2 when AS is activated. Finally, some track all the available codes on both frequencies. In any of these configurations, the GPS surveying receivers that use the P code in combination with the C/A code and/or codeless technology are among the most expensive. Their average cost is approximately $30,000 per unit.

Typical GPS Surveying Receiver Characteristics

These examples represent the general scope of receivers that provide a level of accuracy acceptable for most surveying applications. Most share some practical characteristics: they have multiple independent channels that track the satellites continuously, they begin acquiring satellites' signals from a few seconds to less than a minute from the moment they are switched on. Most acquire all the satellites above their mask angle in a very few minutes, with the time usually lessened by a warm start, and most provide some sort of audible tone to alert the user that data are being recorded. About three-quarters of them can have their sessions preprogrammed in the office before going to their field sites. And nearly all allow the user to select the *sampling rate* of their phase measurements, from 0 to 999 seconds. While there is some variation from receiver to receiver in all these features, they all have one thing in common: though they may track the C/A code for an initial lock, their extraordinary accuracy comes from postprocessing the information they store in their memories.

Handheld GPS Receivers

There is one category of GPS receivers with some surveying application that only track the C/A code. Most of these C/A code pseudorange receivers are small handheld devices, often powered by flashlight batteries. Still, they have several independent channels; they display the same information available from the more expensive receivers, and their civilian use by boaters, hikers, even automobile manufacturers is growing. But unlike more sophisticated receivers, they are not capable of measuring the carrier phase observable. These receivers were developed with the needs of navigation in mind. In fact, they are sometimes categorized by the number of waypoints they can store. (*Waypoint* is a term that grew out of military usage. It means the coordinate of an intermediate position a person, vehicle, or airplane must pass to reach a desired destination. With such a receiver, a navigator may call up a distance and direction from his present location to the next waypoint.) However, for surveying applications, this type of GPS receiver is relatively inaccurate and generally limited to point or differential positioning. These units can cost as little as $2,000 to $3,000, but the average is closer to $10,000.

GPS Receiver Costs

Comparing the cost of GPS receivers over time is complicated by the fact that today, postprocessing software is often included in their prices. Nevertheless, it is clear that the cost of GPS receivers and GPS technology overall has been through a remarkable decline. The first GPS receivers were five times more expensive than the highest-priced receiver available today. At the same time, the capabilities of even an average receiver have come to outstrip those of the best of the early instruments. These trends will undoubtedly continue, but perhaps the more important aspect of receiver development is the increase in their variety. This growth in diversity has been driven by the rapid expansion in the scope of the uses of GPS.

As previously mentioned, the GPS work done in geodetic and land surveying relies on postprocessed relative positioning. There are several very different techniques available to GPS surveyors, and each method makes unique demands on the receivers used to support it.

SOME GPS SURVEYING METHODS

Static

This was the first method of GPS surveying used in the field and it continues to be the primary technique today. Relative static positioning involves several stationary receivers simultaneously collecting data from at least four satellites during observation sessions that usually last from 30 minutes to 2 hours. A typical application of this method would be the determination of vectors, or baselines, as they are called, between several static receivers to accuracies from 1 ppm to 0.1 ppm over tens of kilometers (Table 4.1).

Prerequisites for Static GPS

There are few absolute requirements for relative static positioning. The requisites include: more than one receiver, four or more satellites, and a mostly unobstructed sky above the stations to be occupied. But as

Table 4.1. Methods

Technique	Accuracy	Observation Time	Drawbacks	Strengths
Static	1/100,000 to 1/5,000,000	1 to 2 hr	Slow.	High accuracy.
Kinematic	1/100,000 to 1/750,000	1 to 2 min	Requires constant lock on at least 4 satellites. Needs initialization.	Fast.
Rapid static	1/100,000 to 1/1,000,000	5 to 20 min	Requires the most sophisticated equipment.	Very fast and accurate.
On-the-fly (OTF)	1/100,000 to 1/1,000,000	Virtually instantaneous positioning.	Just emerging from the experimental stage.	Allows highly accurate positions from a receiver in motion.
Pseudokinematic	1/50,000 to 1/500,000	10 to 20 min. 2 observations, 1 to 4 hours apart.	Requires 2 separate observations per point.	More productive than static.

in most of surveying, the rest of the elements of the system are dependent on several other considerations.

Productivity

The assessment of the productivity of a GPS survey almost always hinges, in part at least, on the length of the observation sessions required to satisfy the survey specifications. The determination of the session's duration depends on several particulars, such as the length of the baseline and the relative position, that is the geometry, of the satellites among others (Figure 4.3).

Session Length

Generally speaking, the larger the constellation of satellites, the better the available geometry, the lower the position dilution of precision (PDOP), and the shorter the length of the session needed to achieve the required accuracy. For example, given six satellites and good geometry, baselines of 10 km or less might require a session of 45 minutes to 1 hour, whereas under exactly the same conditions, baselines over 20 km might require a session of 2 hours or more. Alternatively, 45 minutes of six-satellite data may be worth an hour of four-satellite data, depending on the arrangement of the satellites in the sky.

Large Amounts of Data

A static receiver gathers a huge amount of data during an observation session of 1 or 2 hours. Why does it need so much information? The answer may be a bit of a surprise. One might expect there to be some sort of time-consuming process that gradually refines the receiver's measurements down to the last millimeter. The situation is quite different. In fact, the receiver actually achieves the millimeter level of accuracy in a matter of seconds, in as little as a single epoch. It is the resolution of the larger divisions of the measurement, the meters, for example, that require long observation so typical of relative static positioning.

Resolution of the Cycle Ambiguity

The receiver does not need long sessions to make the fine distinctions between millimeters. It needs long sessions to solve the integer number of cycles between itself and the satellites, the so-called *cycle ambiguity* prob-

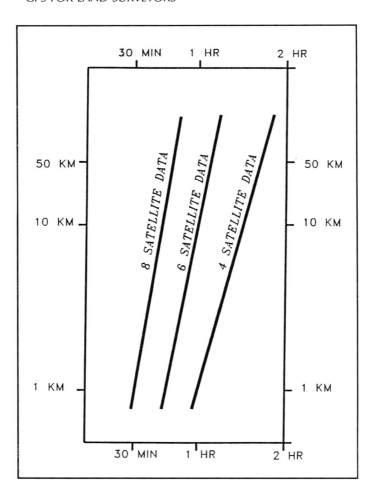

Figure 4.3. Generalized Session Lengths for Static Baselines.

lem. In fact, it is the unique handling of precisely this difficulty that allows the kinematic method to achieve high accuracy with very much shorter occupation times. In the static application, the receivers must resolve the phase ambiguity anew with each occupation, so the sessions are long. But in the kinematic method the receiver resolves the phase ambiguity once, and only once, at the beginning of the project. Then, by keeping a continuous lock on the satellite's signals, it maintains that solution throughout the work. This strategy allows for short occupations without sacrificing accuracy. (Please see Chapter 1 for a more thorough presentation of the cause of the cycle ambiguity problem.)

Preprogrammed Observations

Many receivers offer the user facility to preprogram parameters at the occupied station. Some are so automatic they do not require operator interaction at all once they are programmed and onsite, a feature that can be somewhat of a mixed blessing. This will be investigated in more detail in the section on planning a GPS survey.

Observation Settings

The selection of satellites to track, start, and stop times, mask elevation angle, assignment of a data file name, reference position, bandwidth, and sampling rate are some options useful in the static mode, as well as other GPS surveying methods. These features may appear to be prosaic, but their practicality is not always obvious. For example, satellite selection can seem unnecessary when using a receiver with sufficient independent channels to track all satellites above the receiver's horizon without difficulty. However, it is quite useful when the need arises to eliminate data from a satellite that is known to be unhealthy, before the observation begins.

Data Interval

Another example is the selectable sampling rate, also known as the *data interval*. This feature allows the user to stipulate the short period of time between each of the microprocessor's downloads to storage. The fastest rate available is usually between 0 and 1 second, and the slowest, 999 seconds. The faster the data-sampling rate, the larger the volume of data a receiver collects, and the larger the amount of storage it needs. A fast rate is helpful in cycle slip detection, and that improves the receiver's performance on baselines longer than 50 km, where the detection and repair of cycle slips can be particularly difficult.

Compatible Receivers

Relative static positioning, just as all the subsequent surveying methods discussed here, involves several receivers occupying many sites. Problems can be avoided as long as the receivers on a project are compatible. For example, it is helpful if they have the same number of channels and signal processing techniques.

Receiver Capabilities and Baseline Length

The number and type of channels available to a receiver is a consideration because, generally speaking, the more satellites the receiver can track continuously, the better. Another factor that ought to be weighed is whether a receiver has single or dual-frequency capability. Single-frequency receivers are best applied to relatively short baselines, say, under 25 km. The biases at one end of such a vector are likely to be similar to those at the other. Dual-frequency receivers, on the other hand, have the capability to nearly eliminate the effects of ionospheric refraction, and can handle longer baselines.

Static GPS surveying has the widest application of the current techniques. It has been used on control surveys from local to statewide extent, and will probably continue to be the preferred technique in that category. But it is flexible, making it suitable for surveys from photo-control to deformation studies.

Kinematic

Reference Receiver and Rover Receivers

As previously mentioned, kinematic positioning is faster than the static method. The term *kinematic* is sometimes applied to GPS surveying methods where receivers are in continuous motion, but for relative positioning the more typical arrangement is a stop-and-go technique. This latter approach involves the use of at least one stationary reference receiver and at least one moving receiver, called a *rover*. The technique is similar to static GPS in that all the receivers observe the same satellites simultaneously, and the reference receivers occupy the same control points throughout the survey. However, the kinematic method differs from static GPS in the movement of the rovers from point to point across the network. They stop momentarily at each new point, usually for 2 minutes or less, and their data eventually provide vectors between themselves and the reference receivers.

Leapfrog Kinematic

There is a variation of this technique involving two receivers. It is known as the *leapfrog* approach. Instead of either of the receivers remaining a motionless reference throughout the survey, they both move, one at a time. In its simplest form, the receivers take the roving in turns.

First receiver A is stationary and receiver B moves; then receiver B waits while receiver A moves. But since they never move at the same time, they each take a turn to ensure that at any given moment one of them is providing a static anchor for each vector in the survey, however briefly.

Kinematic Positional Accuracy

When compared with the other relative positioning methods, there is little question that the very short sessions of the kinematic method can produce the largest number of positions in the least amount of time. The remarkable thing is that this technique can do so with only slight degradation in the accuracy of the work. Recall that in static GPS, the long sessions are not required to resolve the finest aspect of the carrier phase measurement. The millimeters are resolved in a matter of seconds. It is the determination of the meters, the resolution of the integer number of cycles or so-called *phase ambiguity*, that takes the time.

Initialization

The kinematic technique avoids this delay by resolving the phase ambiguity before the survey begins, in a process called *initialization* (Figure 4.4). There are at least two ways to accomplish initialization. The receivers can occupy each end of a baseline between two control points and since the distance between the points is known, the phase ambiguity is resolved in a few minutes.

Antenna Swap

Another method is called the *antenna swap*. The antenna swap requires that the two receivers involved are active and collecting data through their antennas from at least four satellites during the entire procedure. One, receiver A, occupies a control point, while the other, receiver B, occupies the first point of the kinematic survey. Obviously, it is also helpful if the two points are conveniently close together.

Following a few minutes of observation the receivers are switched. Receiver A is moved from the control point to the starting point, and receiver B is moved from the starting point to the control point. After another few minutes of observation, they are switched back to their original points. Receiver B is moved from the control point back to the starting point, and receiver A is moved from the starting point back to the

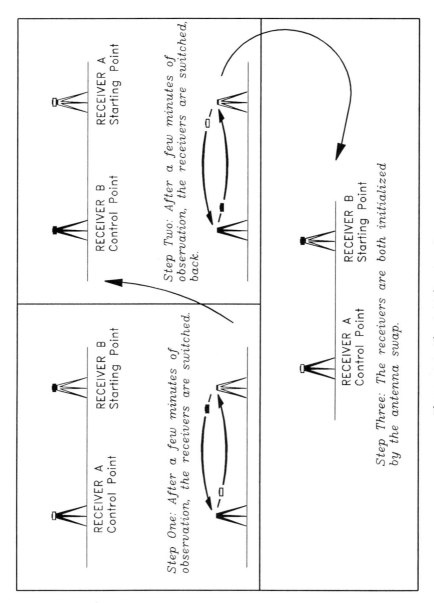

RECEIVER A
Starting Point

RECEIVER B
Control Point

Step Two: After a few minutes of observation, the receivers are switched back.

RECEIVER B
Starting Point

RECEIVER A
Control Point

Step One: After a few minutes of observation, the receivers are switched.

RECEIVER B
Starting Point

RECEIVER A
Control Point

Step Three: The receivers are both initialized by the antenna swap.

Figure 4.4. The Initialization Process.

control point. With typical tribrach-mounted antennas, or receivers with built-in antennas, the antenna swap procedure is fast and easy, since the tribrachs may stay on their tripods and simply be locked and unlocked to accommodate the instruments. After a few minutes of data in their final position the vector between the two points will be determined to millimeter accuracy. With the receivers both initialized, the kinematic survey may begin.

Maintaining Lock

Once the phase ambiguity is resolved with one of these initialization techniques, the receivers are kept running and their lock on the satellites' signals are carefully maintained throughout the survey by avoiding any obstructions that may interrupt them. The drawback of kinematic GPS is that not only must the occupied stations be free of overhead obstructions, the route between them must also be clear. Otherwise the lock could be lost while the roving receiver is moving from point to point, and the initialization procedure would have to be repeated.

Reconnaissance

Therefore, kinematic surveys require considerable reconnaissance. Trees, utility poles, buildings, fences—any sort of structure, natural or man made—that might prevent the satellite's signals from reaching the receiver for even an instant must be avoided to achieve maximum efficiency with the kinematic method. For this reason it is best to consider five, rather than four, satellites to be the absolute minimum number in planning a kinematic survey. Despite the best reconnaissance, the signal from one satellite may easily be lost during the work. If five are considered the minimum from the outset, such a loss is not nearly so disastrous, since four will remain.

Applications

Kinematic GPS has an ever-widening scope, but it is best suited for work done in wide-open areas. Several kinematic procedures are being developed for airborne and marine work, including photogrammetry without ground control. Land-based kinematic relative positioning applications range from gravity field surveys to construction work. Another example might be a vehicle-mounted receiver moving from station to station along cross-sectional lines. This technique could be used to collect data for a highly accurate topographic map of an area.

Kinematic Positioning and Navigation

However, when considering kinematic techniques for a project, it is important to make a distinction between kinematic relative positioning and navigation. While kinematic positioning is similar to navigation in some ways, they are not the same, particularly when it comes to receivers and accuracy.

The primary objectives of navigation applications of GPS are velocity and heading; in short, the dynamics of a receiver's movement. The term *dynamic GPS* or *DGPS* has come to describe such navigational GPS work. But in kinematic GPS, it is the momentary position of the receiver with respect to a three-dimensional coordinate system that is the primary concern. Another difference is that relative kinematic applications depend on postprocessing, while navigational solutions are usually needed in real time. And finally, surveyors generally expect kinematic GPS to provide them with accuracies at the centimeter level. Therefore, the navigational solutions of handheld C/A code-tracking pseudorange receivers have limited application.

Most Carrier Phase Receivers Capable of Kinematic GPS

On the other hand, the majority of the receivers that measure the carrier phase observable are quite adequate to most kinematic applications and generally offer it, along with their static capability. Still, even within that wide selection, some receiver characteristics are more useful than others. For example, a fast data-sampling rate is essential in kinematic surveys. From 1 to 5 seconds is usual, but even faster rates may be needed in work that requires the receivers to be in continuous motion. An option of bandwidth selection in the tracking loops is also helpful in kinematic applications.

Wide-Band

A wide-band signal is transmitted by the GPS satellites because it provides some immunity from jamming and is capable of high-resolution ranging. However, after it has been collected by the receiver, the spread-spectrum signal is usually compressed, or *despread*, into a smaller bandwidth by demodulating it with an identical wideband waveform. Having the option to select the bandwidth is helpful because the narrower it is, the better the signal-to-noise ratio *(SNR)*. But there is a tradeoff; although the SNR for the narrower bandwidth is better, a wider bandwidth provides a more secure signal lock. In the end, receivers that can be adapted to find the best balance provide the best results.

Practical Considerations in Kinematic GPS

The physical characteristics of the receiver also need to be considered. When the work is likely to encounter heavy vegetation, a receiver with a separate antenna is a boon, particularly in the kinematic mode. Mounted on a range pole or mast, it can sometimes be elevated above the obstructions.

In kinematic work where the equipment must be packed in, two obvious factors in determining a receiver's suitability are its weight and rate of power consumption. A receiver that provides the user with an audible warning when lock is lost is also quite useful in kinematic applications. This feature may help a user avoid the continuation of a kinematic survey that must be reinitialized. Along the same line, it is a good idea to perform a second antenna swap or other reinitialization procedure at the close of a kinematic survey as a bit of insurance. Then, if a loss of lock did occur during the observations, the data may still be rescued by running the postprocessing in reverse, from the closing initialization.

Pseudokinematic

This technique has several names. It has come to be known as *pseudokinematic*, *pseudostatic*, and *intermittent-static*. The variety in its titles is indicative of its standing between static and kinematic in terms of productivity. It is less productive than kinematic, but more productive than the static method. While it is also somewhat less accurate than either relative static or kinematic positioning, its primary advantage is its flexibility. There is no need for the receiver to maintain a lock on the satellite's signals while moving from station to station.

Double Occupation

The pseudokinematic observation procedures can be virtually identical to those previously described for the kinematic relative positioning.

However, there is a fundamental difference between the two. In pseudokinematic work, it is necessary to occupy the unknown stations twice. Each one of the two occupations may be as brief as 5 or 10 minutes, but they should be separated by at least 1 hour and not more than 4 hours. The time between the two occupations allows the satellites of the second session to reach a configuration different enough from that of the first, for resolution of the phase ambiguity. This removes the necessity of maintaining a constant lock on the satellite's signals, as required in kinematic work. It also allows the user to occupy many more stations than would be possible with static positioning over the same time.

No Need for Continuous Lock

In pseudokinematic relative positioning, at least two stationary receivers collect up to 10 minutes of data from the same satellites at the same time. A different baseline is occupied by moving one or both of the receivers, without continuous lock. In fact, the receivers may even be switched off during the move. After the move they collect up to 10 minutes of data from the ends of the new baseline. This procedure continues until all of the baselines have been occupied. So far the method is very like other relative positioning techniques, but pseudokinematic differs from the others in that, following the initial occupations, the receivers must return to every one of the baselines in the same manner a second time.

Best Used in Easy Access Situations

While the accuracy of the technique is usually at the subcentimeter level, the production advantage of the procedure over the static mode is somewhat diminished by the reoccupation requirement. Therefore, the best application of pseudokinematic GPS is over relatively short baselines, under 10 km, where the access to the stations is quick and easy.

Mostly Radial Surveys

The majority of receivers that measure the carrier phase observable offer both kinematic and pseudokinematic surveying along with their static capability. Pseudokinematic, as well as kinematic, procedures tend to encourage radial surveys. While the radial approach may be useful for mapping, topography, photocontrol, and some low-order mining surveys; its open-ended quality may not be adequate in other work, like control surveys.

Rapid-Static

Also known as *fast-static*, this field procedure is like pseudokinematic in that it can succeed with very short occupation times. However, it is unlike pseudokinematic in that baselines positioned with rapid-static need be occupied only once. Neither does this procedure require continuous lock on the satellite's signals, as does the kinematic method.

Wide Laning

These advantages are accomplished by relying on the sophisticated hardware of the most expensive receivers. Success in rapid-static depends on the use of receivers that can combine code and carrier phase measurements from both GPS frequencies. The field procedures in rapid-static are very like those of the static method. But using a technique known as *wide laning*, rapid-static can provide the user with nearly the same accuracy available from 1- and 2-hour sessions of relative static positioning with observations of 5 to 20 minutes.

Wide laning is based on the linear combination of the measured phases from both GPS frequencies, L1 and L2. Carrier phase measurements can be made on L1 and L2 separately, of course, but when they are combined, two distinct signals result. One is called a *narrow lane* and has a short wavelength of 10.7 cm. The other is known as the *wide lane*. Its frequency, only 347.82 MHz, is more than three times slower than the original carriers. Furthermore, its 86.2 cm wavelength is much longer than the 19.0 cm and 24.4 cm of L1 and L2, respectively. These changes greatly increase the spacing of the phase ambiguity, thereby making its resolution much easier.

High-End Receivers

Less than a third of the receivers that measure the carrier phase observable, generally the more expensive models, can be used to do rapid static work. Most are dual-frequency receivers that track both the P code and the C/A code. First, they use smoothed P code pseudoranges to resolve the integer ambiguity of the combined wide lane wavelength, L1/L2. And the resulting solution can then be used to help solve the integer ambiguities of the original base carriers, L1 and L2. But this rapid initialization can only be accomplished by receivers that combine code and carrier phase measurements on both frequencies.

On-the-Fly

Wide laning is also at the heart of a GPS surveying technique called *on-the-fly (OTF)*. This method allows initialization while the receiver is actually in motion.

Accurate Initial Positions

Just as in the rapid-static method, P code pseudoranges provide for the wide-lane integer bias resolution. That solution is then used, in turn, to solve the base carrier's integer ambiguity. The OTF process differs from rapid static in that the P code pseudoranges are electronically refined. At the top of the ambiguity resolution process, several consecutive P code pseudoranges are run through a Kalman filter, a kind of averaging process. This improves the initial position from which the wide-lane and base carrier solutions work, giving the receiver a very accurate, virtually instantaneous idea of where it is. The high-quality starting point makes phase ambiguity resolution very fast.

In fact, these improved P code pseudoranges offer the user an initialization process that is so fast and accurate it can be accomplished while the receiver is in continuous motion. If the receiver momentarily loses lock on the satellite's signals, with OTF the lock can be reacquired without stopping.

Photogrammetry Without Ground Control

The accuracy of OTF is comparable with kinematic GPS, and it lends itself to radial surveys, but it is not crippled by momentary loss of four-satellite data. OTF is a great boon to aerial and hydrographic work, and will likely make the prospect of photogrammetry without ground control a reality, and that is only the beginning of the possible applications of this method.

REFERENCES

Langley, R.B. "The GPS Receiver: An Introduction," *GPS World,* 2(1):50–53 (1991).

Chapter Five

Coordinates

A FEW PERTINENT IDEAS ABOUT GEODETIC DATUMS FOR GPS

Plane Surveying

Plane surveying has traditionally relied on an imaginary flat reference surface, or *datum*, with Cartesian axes. This rectangular system is used to describe measured positions by ordered pairs, usually expressed in northings and eastings, or x- and y- coordinates. Even though surveyors have always known that this assumption of a flat earth is fundamentally unrealistic, it provided, and continues to provide, an adequate arrangement for small areas. The attachment of elevations to such horizontal coordinates somewhat acknowledges the actual topographic irregularity, but the whole system is always undone by its inherent inaccuracy as surveys grow larger.

Development of State Plane Coordinate Systems

In the '30s, an engineer in North Carolina's highway department appealed to the then United States Coast and Geodetic Survey (USC&GS, now NGS) for help. He had found that the stretching and compression

111

inevitable in the representation of the curved earth on a plane was so severe over his long-route surveys that he could not check into the USC&GS geodetic control stations across his state within reasonable limits. To alleviate the problem, Dr. O.S. Adams of the Division of Geodesy designed the first state plane coordinate system in 1933. The approach was so successful in North Carolina that similar systems had been devised for all the states in the Union within a year or so.

The purpose of the state plane coordinate system was to overcome some of the limitations of the horizontal plane datum while avoiding the imposition of geodetic methods and calculations on local surveyors. Using the conic and cylindrical models of the Lambert and Mercator map projections, the flat datum was curved, but only in one direction. By curving the datums and limiting the area of the zones, Dr. Adams managed to limit the distortion to a scale ratio of about 1 part in 10,000 without disturbing the traditional system of ordered pairs of Cartesian coordinates familiar to surveyors.

The state plane coordinate system was a step ahead at that time. To this day, it provides surveyors with a mechanism for coordination of surveying stations that approximates geodetic accuracy more closely than the commonly used methods of small-scale plane surveying. However, the state plane coordinate systems were organized in a time of generally lower accuracy and efficiency in surveying measurement. Its calculations were designed to avoid the lengthy and complicated mathematics of geodesy. It was an understandable compromise in an age when such computation required sharp pencils, logarithmic tables, and lots of midnight oil.

GPS Surveyors and Geodesy

Today, GPS has thrust surveyors into the thick of geodesy, which is no longer the exclusive realm of distant experts. Thankfully, in the age of the microcomputer, the computational drudgery can be handled with software packages. Nevertheless, it is unwise to venture into GPS believing that knowledge of the basics of geodesy is, therefore, unnecessary. It is true that GPS would be impossible without computers, but blind reliance on the data they generate eventually leads to disaster.

Some Geodetic Coordinate Systems

3D Cartesian Coordinates

A spatial Cartesian system with three axes lends itself to describing the terrestrial positions derived from space-based geodesy. Using three rectangular coordinates instead of two, one can unambiguously define any posi-

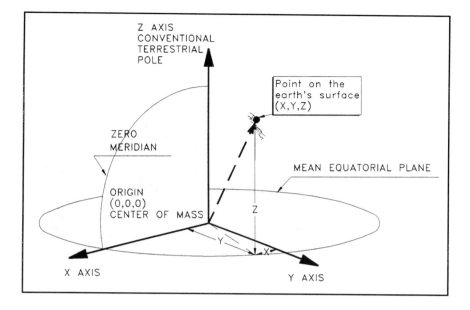

Figure 5.1. Conventional Terrestrial System (CTS) Earth-Centered-Earth-Fixed Coordinate System (ECEF).

tion on the earth, or above it, for that matter. But such a system is only useful if its origin (0,0,0) and its axes (x,y,z) can be fixed to the planet with certainty, something which is easier said than done (Figure 5.1).

The usual arrangement is known as the *conventional terrestrial system (CTS)*. The origin is the center of mass of the earth, the *geocenter*. The *x*-axis is a line from the geocenter through the intersection of the Greenwich meridian with the equator. The *y*-axis is extended from the geocenter along a line perpendicular from the *x*-axis in the same mean equatorial plane. They both rotate with the earth as part of a *right-handed* orthogonal system.

A three-dimensional Cartesian coordinate system is right-handed if it can be described by the following model: the extended forefinger of the right hand symbolizes the positive direction of the *x*-axis. The middle finger of the same hand extended at right angles to the forefinger symbolizes the positive direction of the *y*-axis. The extended thumb of the right hand, perpendicular to them both, symbolizes the positive direction of the *z*-axis. In applying this model to the earth, the *z*-axis is imagined to nearly coincide with the earth's axis of rotation, and therein lies the difficulty.

Polar Motion

The earth's rotational axis will not hold still. It actually wanders slightly with respect to the solid earth in a very slow oscillation called *polar motion*. The largest component of the movement relative to the earth's crust has a 430-day cycle known as the *Chandler period*. The actual displacement caused by the wandering generally does not exceed 12 meters. Nevertheless, the conventional terrestrial system of coordinates would be useless if its third axis was constantly wobbling. Therefore, an average stable position was chosen for the position of the pole and the *z*-axis.

Between 1900 and 1905, the mean position of the earth's rotational pole was designated as the *Conventional International Origin (CIO)*. Using very long baseline interferometry (VLBI) and satellite laser ranging (SLR), it has since been refined by the *International Earth Rotation Service (IERS)*. The name has been changed to the *Conventional Terrestrial Pole (CTP)*, but its role has remained the same; also the CTP provides a stable and clear definition on the earth's surface for the *z*-axis. By international agreement, the *z*-axis of the *Conventional Terrestrial System (CTS)* is a line from the earth's center of mass through the CTP.

The CTS in GPS Postprocessing

The three-dimensional Cartesian coordinates (x,y,z) derived from this system are sometimes known as *earth-centered-earth-fixed (ECEF)* coordinates. They are convenient for many types of calculations, such as the single-baseline or single-vector solution in GPS. In fact, most modern GPS software provide data that express vectors as the difference between the *x, y,* and *z* coordinates at each end of the baselines. The display of these differences as *DX, DY,* and *DZ* is a typical product of these postprocessed calculations (Figure 5.2).

Latitude and Longitude

Despite their utility, such 3-D Cartesian coordinates are not the most common method of expressing a geodetic position. Latitude and longitude have been the coordinates of choice for centuries. The application of these angular designations rely on the same two standard lines as 3-D Cartesian coordinates: the mean equator and the Greenwich meridian. Unlike the CTS, they require some clear representation of the terrestrial surface. In modern practice, latitude and longitude cannot be said to uniquely define a position without a clear definition of the earth itself.

Elements of a Geodetic Datum

How can latitude, ϕ, and longitude, λ, be considered inadequate in any way for the definition of a position on the earth? The reference lines—the mean equator and the Greenwich meridian—are clearly defined. The units of degrees, minutes, seconds, and decimals of seconds, allow for the finest distinctions of measurement. Finally, the reference surface is the earth itself.

Despite the certainty of the physical surface of the earth, it remains notoriously difficult to define in mathematical terms. The dilemma is illustrated by the ancient struggle to represent its curved surface on flat maps. There have been a whole variety of map projections developed over the centuries that rely on mathematical relationships between positions on the earth's surface and points on the map. Each projection serves a particular application well, but none of them can represent the earth without distortion. For example, no modern surveyor would presume to promise a client a high-precision control network with data scaled from a map.

As the technology of measurement has improved, the pressure for greater exactness in the definition of the earth's shape has increased. Even with electronic tools that widen the scope and increase the precision of the data, perfection is nowhere in sight. Still, geodesy builds on a firm foundation.

Development of the Ellipsoidal Model

Despite the fact that local topography is the most obvious feature of the *lithosphere* to an observer standing on the earth, efforts to grasp the more general nature of the planet's shape and size have been occupying scientists for at least 2,300 years. There have, of course, been long intervening periods of unmitigated nonsense on the subject. Ever since 200 B.C. when Eratosthenes almost calculated the planet's circumference correctly, geodesy has been getting ever closer to expressing the actual shape of the earth in numerical terms. A leap forward occurred with Newton's thesis that the earth was an ellipsoid rather than a sphere in the first edition of his *Principia* in 1687.

Newton's idea that the actual shape of the earth was slightly ellipsoidal was not entirely independent. There had already been some other suggestive observations. For example, 15 years earlier astronomer J. Richter had found that to maintain the accuracy of the one-second clock he used in his observations in Cayenne, French Guiana, he had to shorten its pendulum significantly. The clock's pendulum, regulated in Paris, tended to

Project Name: sandlake
Processed: Thursday, December 16, 1993 10:50

Summary Reference Index: WAVE Baseline Processor, version 1.10d
                                           2.6

Fixed Station: 9001
Data file: 17093481.DAT
Antenna Height (meters):   1.667 True Vertical
Position Quality: Fixed Control

WGS 84 Position: 45° 28' 29.825560" N   X -2495069.154
                                           123° 50' 35.633850" W   Y -3721013.198
                                           -15.552   Z 4524506.410

Floating Station: 0001
Data file: 17403482.DAT
Antenna Height (meters):   1.584 True Vertical

WGS 84 Position: 45° 19' 17.804651" N   X -2501621.452
                                           123° 50' 23.033611" W   Y -3731277.694
                                           42.002   Z 4512580.880

Start Time: 12/14/93 23:24:45 GPS   (727 257085)
Stop Time: 12/14/93 23:55:15 GPS   (727 258915)
Occupation Time: 00:30:30.00
Measurement Epoch Interval (seconds):   15:00

Solution Time: Receiver/satellite double difference
                                      Iono free fixed

Solution Acceptability:
Baseline Slope Distance   Std. Dev. (meters):
                                      Passed ratio test
                                      17044.376   0.000574

Normal Section Azimuth:
                    Forward   Backward
                    179° 04' 38.886169"   359° 04' 47.857511"
                    0° 07 00.456589"   -0° 16' 12.548396"

Baseline Components (meters):
dn -17042.131   de 274.423   du 34.744

Standard Deviations:
dx -6552.297   dy -10264.496   dz -11925.530
8.437168E-004   1.072974E-003   9.513724E-004

Aposteriori Covariance Matrix:
7.118580E-007
7.389287E-007   1.151273E-006
-6.141036E-007   -7.690377E-007   9.051094E-007

Variance Ratio   Cutoff:
62.1   1.5
Reference Variance:
0.556

Observable   Count/Rejected   RMS:
Iono free phase   451/0   0.006

Figure 5.2. Differences as DX, DY, and DZ.

swing more slowly as it approached the equator. Newton reasoned that the phenomenon was attributable to a lessening of the force of gravity. Based on his own theoretical work, he explained the weaker gravity by the proposition, "the earth is higher under the equator than at the poles, and that by an excess of about 17 miles" (*Philosophiae naturalis principia mathematica,* Book III, Proposition XX).

Although Newton's model of the planet bulging along the equator and flattened at the poles was supported by some of his contemporaries, notably Huygens, the inventor of Richter's clock, it was attacked by others. The director of the Paris Observatory, Jean Dominique Cassini, for example, took exception with Newton's concept. Even though the elder Cassini had himself observed the flattening of the poles of Jupiter in 1666, neither he nor his equally learned son Jacques were prepared to accept the same idea when it came to the shape of the earth. It appeared they had some empirical evidence on their side.

For geometric verification of the earth model, scientists had employed arc measurements at various latitudes since the early 1500s. Establishing the latitude of their beginning and ending points astronomically, they measured a cardinal line to discover the length of one degree of longitude along a meridian arc. Early attempts assumed a spherical earth and the results were used to estimate its radius by simple multiplication. In fact, one of the most accurate of the measurements of this type, completed in 1670 by the French abbé J. Picard, was actually used by Newton in formulating his own law of gravitation. However, Cassini noted that close analysis of Picard's arc measurement, and others, seemed to show the length of one degree of longitude actually *decreased* as it proceeded northward. He concluded that the earth was not flattened as proposed by Newton, but was rather elongated at the poles.

The argument was not resolved until two expeditions sponsored by the Paris Académie Royale des Sciences produced irrefutable proof. One group, which included Clairaut and Maupertuis, was sent to measure a meridian arc near the Arctic Circle, 66°20' Nϕ, in Lapland. Another expedition with Bouguer and Godin, to what is now Ecuador, measured an arc near the equator, 01°31' Sϕ. Newton's conjecture was proved correct, and the contradictory evidence of Picard's arc was charged to errors in the latter's measurement of the astronomic latitudes.

The ellipsoidal model (Figure 5.3), bulging at the equator and flattened at the poles, has been used ever since as a representation of the general shape of the earth's surface. In fact, several reference ellipsoids have been established for various regions of the planet. They are precisely defined by their semi-major axis and flattening. The relationship between these parameters are expressed in the formula:

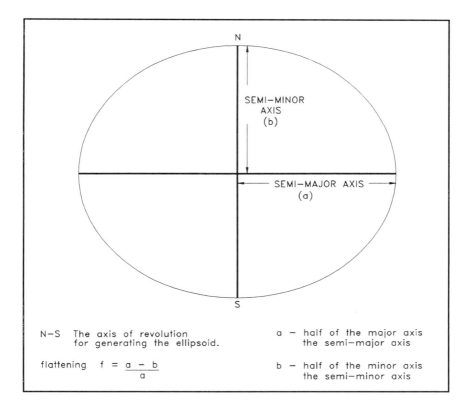

Figure 5.3. Ellipsoidal Model of the Earth.

$$f = \frac{a-b}{a}$$

where f = flattening,
       a = semi-major axis, and
       b = semi-minor axis.

The Role of an Ellipsoid in a Datum

The semi-major and flattening can be used to completely define an ellipsoid. However, six additional elements are required if that ellipsoid is to be used as a *geodetic datum:* three to specify its center and three more to clearly indicate its orientation around that center. The *Clarke 1866 spheroid* is one of many reference ellipsoids. Its shape is completely defined by a semimajor axis, *a*, of 6378.2064 km and a flattening, *f*, of 1/

294.9786982. It is the reference ellipsoid of the datum known to surveyors as the *North American Datum of 1927 (NAD27)*, but it is not the datum itself.

For the Clarke 1866 spheroid to become NAD27, it had to be attached at a point and specifically oriented to the actual surface of the earth. However, even this ellipsoid, which best fits North America, could not conform to that surface perfectly. Therefore, the initial point was chosen near the center of the anticipated geodetic network to best distribute the inevitable distortion. The attachment was established at Meades Ranch, Kansas, 39°13'26".686 Nϕ, 98°32'30".506 Wλ and *geoidal height* zero (we will discuss geoidal height later). Those coordinates were not sufficient, however. The establishment of directions from this initial point was required to complete the orientation. The azimuth from Meades Ranch to station Waldo was fixed at 75°28'09".64 and the deflection of the vertical set at zero (more later about the deflection of the vertical).

Once the initial point and directions were fixed, the whole orientation of NAD27 was established, including the center of the reference ellipsoid. Its center was imagined to reside somewhere around the center of mass of the earth. However, the two points were certainly not coincident, nor were they intended to be. In short, NAD27 does not employ a geocentric ellipsoid.

Measurement Technology and Datum Selection

In the period before space-based geodesy was tenable, such a regional datum was not unusual. The *Australian Geodetic Datum 1966*, the *Datum Eurpeén 1950*, and the *South American Datum 1969*, among others, were also designed as nongeocentric systems. Achievement of the minimum distortion over a particular region was the primary consideration in choosing their ellipsoids, not the relationship of their centers to the center of mass of the earth (Figure 5.4). For example, in the Conventional Terrestrial System (CTS), the 3-D Cartesian coordinates of the center of the Clarke 1866 spheroid as it was used for NAD27 are about X = -4 m, Y = +166 m and Z = +183 m.

This approach to the design of datums was bolstered by the fact that the vast majority of geodetic measurements they would be expected to support were of the classical variety. That is, the work was done with theodolites, towers, and tapes. They were, in short, earthbound. Even after the advent of electronic distance measurement, the general approach involved the determination of horizontal coordinates by measuring from point to point on the earth's surface and adding heights, otherwise known as *elevations*, through a separate leveling operation. As long as this meth-

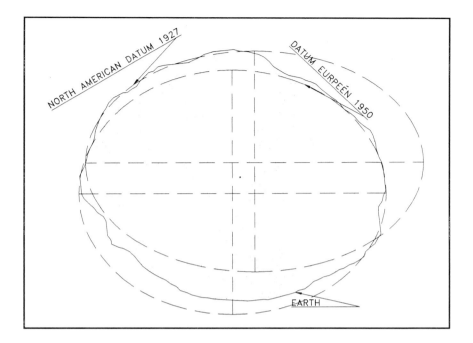

Figure 5.4. Regional Datums.

odological separation existed between the horizontal and vertical coordinates of a station, the difference between the ellipsoid and the true earth's surface was not an overriding concern. Such circumstances did not require a geocentric datum.

However, as the sophistication of satellite geodesy increased, the need for a truly global, geocentric datum became obvious. The horizontal and vertical information were no longer separate. Since satellites orbit around the center of mass of the earth, a position derived from space-based geodesy can be visualized as a vector originating from that point.

So, today, not only are the horizontal and vertical components of a position derived from precisely the same vector, the choice of the coordinate system used to express them is actually a matter of convenience. The position vector can be transformed into the 3D Cartesian system of CTS, the traditional latitude, longitude, and height, or virtually any other well-defined coordinate system. However, since the orbital motion and the subsequent position vector derived from satellite geodesy are themselves earth-centered, it follows that the most straightforward representations of that data are earth-centered as well (Figure 5.5).

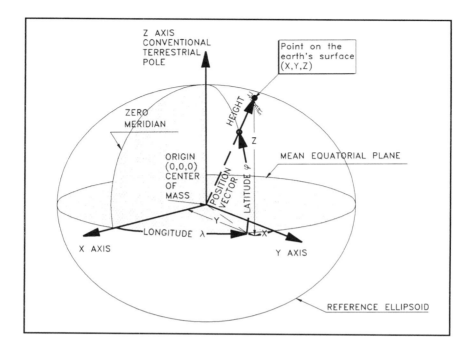

Figure 5.5. A Position Derived from Space-Base Geodesy Visualized as a
Vector Originating from That Point.

The Development of a Geocentric Model

Satellites have not only provided the impetus for a geocentric datum, they have also supplied the means to achieve it. In fact, the orbital perturbations of man-made near-earth satellites have probably
brought more refinements to the understanding of the shape of the
earth in a shorter span of time than was ever before possible. For
example, the analysis of the precession of Sputnik 2 in the late '50s
showed researchers that the earth's semi-minor axis was actually 85
meters shorter than had been previously thought. In 1958, while study-
ing the tracking data from the orbit of Vanguard I, Ann Bailey of the
Goddard Spaceflight Center discovered that the planet is shaped a bit
like a pear. There is a slight protuberance at the North Pole, a little
depression at the South Pole, and a small bulge just south of the equator.

These formations and others have been discovered through the
observation of small distortions in satellites' otherwise elliptical orbits,

little bumps in their road, so to speak. The deviations are caused by the action of earth's gravity on the satellites as they travel through space. Just as Richter's clock reacted to the lessening of gravity at the equator and thereby revealed one of the largest features of the earth's shape to Newton, small perturbations in the orbits of satellites, also responding to gravity, reveal details of earth's shape to today's scientists. The common aspect of these examples is the direct relationship between direction and magnitude of gravity and the planet's form. In fact, the surface that best fits the earth's gravity field has been given a name. It is called the *geoid*.

The Geoid

An often-used description of the geoidal surface involves idealized oceans. Imagine the oceans of the world utterly still, completely free of currents, tides, friction, variations in temperature and all other physical forces, except gravity. Reacting to gravity alone, these unattainable calm waters would coincide with the figure known as the geoid. Admitted by small frictionless channels or tubes and allowed to migrate across the land, the water would then, theoretically, define the same geoidal surface across the continents, too.

Of course, the 70 percent of the earth covered by oceans is not so cooperative, nor is there any such system of channels and tubes. In addition, the physical forces eliminated from the model cannot be avoided in reality. These unavoidable forces actually cause mean sea level to deviate up to 1, even 2, meters from the geoid, a fact frequently mentioned to emphasize the inconsistency of the original definition of the geoid as it was offered by J.B. Listing in 1872. Listing thought of the geoidal surface as equivalent to mean sea level. Even though his idea does not stand up to scrutiny today, it can still be instructive.

An Equipotential Surface

Gravity is not consistent across the topographic surface of the earth. At every point it has a magnitude and a direction. In other words, anywhere on the earth, gravity can be described by a mathematical vector. Along the solid earth, such vectors do not have all the *same* direction or magnitude, but one can imagine a surface of constant gravity potential. Such an *equipotential* surface would be *level* in the true sense. It would coincide with the top of the hypothetical water in the previous example. Despite the fact that real mean sea level does not define such a figure, the geoidal surface is not just a product of imagination. For example, the vertical axis of any properly leveled surveying instrument and the string of any stable plumb bob are perpendicular to the geoid. Just as pendulum clocks and earth-orbiting satellites, they clearly show that the geoid is a physical reality.

Geoidal Undulation

Just as the geoid does not precisely follow mean sea level, neither does it exactly correspond with the topography of the dry land. However, it is irregular similar to the terrestrial surface. It has similar peaks and valleys. It is bumpy. Uneven distribution of the mass of the planet makes it maddeningly so. Maddening, because if the solid earth had no internal anomalies of density, the geoid would be smooth and almost exactly ellipsoidal. In that case, the reference ellipsoid could fit the geoid to near perfection, and the lives of geodesists would be much simpler. But like the earth itself, the geoid defies such mathematical consistency and departs from true ellipsoidal form by as much as 100 meters in places (Figure 5.6).

The Modern Geocentric Datum

Three distinct figures are involved in a geodetic datum for latitude, longitude, and height: the geoid, the reference ellipsoid, and the earth itself. Due in large measure to the ascendancy of satellite geodesy, it has become highly desirable that they share a common center.

While the closed level surface of the geoid provides a solid foundation for the definitions of heights (more about that later) and the topographic surface of the Earth is necessarily where measurements are made, neither can serve as the reference surface for geodetic position determinations. From the continents to the floors of the oceans, the solid earth's actual surface is too irregular to be represented by a simple mathematical relation. The geoid, which is sometimes under, and sometimes above, the surface of the earth, has an overall shape that also defies any concise geometrical definition. The ellipsoid, on the other hand, not only has the same general shape as the earth, but, unlike the other two figures, can be described simply and completely in mathematical terms.

Therefore, a global geocentric system has been developed based on the ellipsoid adopted by the *International Union of Geodesy and Geophysics (IUGG)* in 1979. It is called the *Geodetic Reference System 1980 (GRS80)*. Its semi-major axis, a, is 6378.137 km and is probably within a

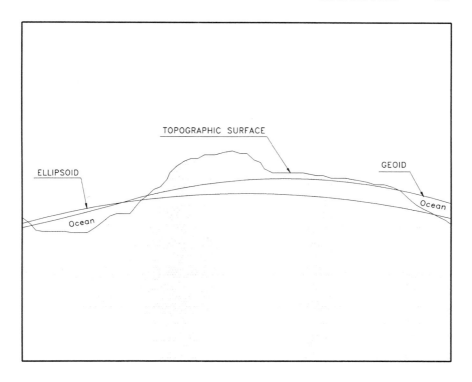

Figure 5.6. The Geoid Departs from True Ellipsoidal Form in Places.

couple of meters of the earth's actual equatorial radius. Its flattening, *f*, is 1/298.25722 and likely deviates only slightly from the true value, a considerable improvement over Newton's calculation of a flattening ratio of 1/230. But then, he did not have orbital data from near-earth satellites to check his work.

With very slight changes, GRS80 is the reference ellipsoid for the coordinate system, known as the *World Geodetic System 1984 (WGS84)*. This datum has been used by the U.S. military since January 21, 1987, as the basis for the GPS Navigation message computations. Therefore, coordinates provided directly by GPS receivers are based in WGS84. However, most available GPS software can transform those coordinates to a number of other datums as well. The one that is probably of greatest interest to surveyors in the United States today is the *North American Datum 1983 (NAD83)*. But the difference between WGS84 and NAD83 coordinates is so small, usually about the 0.1-mm level, that transformation is unnecessary and they can be considered equivalent for most applications.

NAD83

NAD27

The Clarke 1866 ellipsoid was the foundation of NAD27, and the blocks that built that foundation were made by geodetic triangulation. After all, an ellipsoid, even one with a clearly stated orientation to the earth, is only an abstraction until physical, identifiable control stations are available for its practical application. During the tenure of NAD27, control positions were tied together by triangulation. Its measurements grew into chains of figures from Canada to Mexico and coast to coast, with their vertices perpetuated by bronze disks set in stone, concrete, and other permanent media.

These tri-stations, also known as brass caps, and their attached coordinates have provided a framework for all types of surveying and mapping projects for many years. They have served to locate international, state, and county boundaries. They have provided geodetic control for the planning of national and local projects, development of natural resources, national defense, and land management. They have enabled surveys to be fitted together, provided checks, and assisted in the perpetuation of their marks. They have supported scientific inquiry, including crustal monitoring studies and other geophysical research. But even as application of the nationwide control network grew, the revelations of local distortions in NAD27 were reaching unacceptable levels.

Judged by the standards of newer measurement technologies, the quality of some of the observations used in the datum were too low. That, and its lack of an internationally viable geocentric ellipsoid, finally drove its positions to obsolescence. The monuments remain, but it was clear as early as 1970 that the NAD27 coordinates of the national geodetic control network were no longer adequate.

The Development of the New Datum

Work on the new datum, NAD83, did not really begin until 1975. Leading the charge was an old agency with a new name, the same one that had administered NAD27. Once the *United States Coast and Geodetic Survey (USC&GS)*, the agency is now known as the *National Geodetic Survey (NGS)*. It is within the *National Oceanic and Atmospheric Administration (NOAA)*. The first ancestor of today's NGS was established back in 1807 and was known as the *Survey of the Coast*. Its current authority is contained in United States Code, Title 33, USC 883a.

The NGS and the Geodetic Survey of Canada set about the task of attaching and orienting the GRS80 ellipsoid to the actual surface of the earth, as it was defined by the best positions available at the time. It took more than 10 years to readjust and redefine the horizontal coordinate system of North America into what is now NAD83. More than 1.75 million positions derived from classical surveying techniques throughout the Western Hemisphere were involved in the least-squares adjustment. They were supplemented by approximately 30,000 EDM measured baselines, 5,000 astronomic azimuths, and 800 Doppler stations positioned by the TRANSIT satellite system. Very Long Baseline Interferometry (VLBI) vectors were also included. But GPS, in its infancy, contributed only five points.

GPS was growing up in the early '80s, and some of the agencies involved in its development decided to join forces. NOAA, the *National Aeronautics and Space Administration (NASA)*, the *United States Geological Survey (USGS),* and the Department of Defense coordinated their efforts. As a result, each agency was assigned specific responsibilities. NGS was charged with the development of specifications for GPS operations, investigation of related technologies, and the use of GPS for modeling crustal motion. It was also authorized to conduct its subsequent geodetic control surveys with GPS. So, despite an initial sparseness of GPS data in the creation of NAD83, the stage was set for a systematic infusion of its positions as the datum matured.

The Management of NAD83

With the surveying capability of GPS and the new NAD83 reference system in place, NGS began the long process of a nationwide upgrade of their control networks. Now known as the *National Geodetic Reference System (NGRS)*, it actually includes three networks. A horizontal network provides geodetic latitudes and longitudes in the North American Datums. A vertical network furnishes heights, also known as elevations, in the *National Geodetic Vertical Datums (NGVD)*. A gravity network supplies gravity values in the U.S. absolute gravity reference system. Any particular station may have its position defined in one, two, or all three networks.

NGS is computing and publishing NAD83 values for monumented stations, old and new, throughout the United States. Gradually, the new information will provide the common- coordinate basis that is so important to all surveying and mapping activities. But the pace of such a major overhaul must be deliberate, and a significant number of stations will still have only NAD27 positions for some time to come. This unevenness in the upgrade from NAD27 to NAD83 causes a recurrent problem to GPS surveyors across the country.

Since geodetic accuracy with GPS depends on relative positioning, surveyors continue to rely on NGS stations to control their work just as they have for generations. Today, it is not unusual for surveyors to find that some NGS stations have published coordinates in NAD83, and others, perhaps needed to control the same project, only have positions in NAD27. In such a situation, it is often desirable to transform the NAD27 positions into coordinates of the newer datum. But, unfortunately, there is no single-step mathematical approach that can do it accurately.

The distortions between the original NAD27 positions are part of the difficulty. The older coordinates were sometimes in error as much as 1 part in 15,000. Problems stemming from neglect of the deflection of the vertical, lack of correction for geoidal undulations, low-quality measurements, and other sources contributed to inaccuracies in some NAD27 coordinates that cannot be corrected by simply transforming them into another datum.

Transformations from NAD27 to NAD83

Nevertheless, various approximate methods are used to transform NAD27 coordinates into supposed NAD83 values. For example, the computation of a constant local translation is sometimes attempted using stations with coordinates in both systems as a guide. Another technique is the calculation of two translations, one rotation and one scale parameter, for particular locations based on the latitudes and longitudes of three or more common stations. Perhaps the best results derive from polynomial expressions developed for coordinate differences, expressed in Cartesian $(\Delta x, \Delta y, \Delta z)$ or ellipsoidal coordinates $(\Delta\phi, \Delta\lambda, \Delta h)$, using a 3-D Helmert transformation. However, besides requiring seven parameters (three shift, one scale, and three rotation components), this approach is at its best when ellipsoidal heights are available for all the points involved. Where adequate information is available, software packages such as the NGS programs LEFTI or NADCON can provide geodetic quality coordinates.

Even if a local transformation is modeled with these techniques, the resulting NAD27 positions might still be plagued with relatively low accuracy. The NAD83 adjustment of the national network is based on nearly 10 times the number of observations that supported the NAD27 system. This larger quantity of data, combined with the generally higher quality of the measurements at the foundation of NAD83, can have some rather unexpected results. For example, when NAD27 coordinates are transformed into the new system, the shift of individual stations may be quite different from what the regional trend indicates. In short, when using control from both NAD83 and NAD27 simultaneously on the same project, surveyors have come to expect difficulty.

In fact, the only truly reliable method of transformation is not to rely on coordinates at all, but to return to the original observations themselves. It is important to remember, for example, that geodetic latitude and longitude, as other coordinates, are specifically referenced to a given datum and are not derived from some sort of absolute framework. But the original measurements, incorporated into a properly designed least-squares adjustment, can provide most satisfactory results.

Densification and Improvement of NAD83

The inadequacies of NAD27 and even NAD83 positions in some regions, are growing pains of a fundamentally changed relationship. In the past, relatively few engineers and surveyors were employed in geodetic work. Perhaps the greatest importance of the data from the various geodetic surveys was that they furnished precise points of reference to which the multitude of surveys of lower precision could then be tied. This arrangement was clearly illustrated by the design of state plane coordinates systems, devised to make the national control network accessible to surveyors without geodetic capability.

However, the situation has changed. The gulf between the precision of local surveys and national geodetic work is virtually closed by GPS, and that has changed the relationship between local surveyors in private practice and geodesists. For example, the significance of state plane coordinates as a bridge between the two groups has been drastically reduced. Today's surveyor has relatively easy and direct access to the geodetic coordinate systems themselves through GPS. In fact, the 1- to 2-ppm probable error in networks of relative GPS-derived positions frequently exceeds the accuracy of the first-order NAD83 positions intended to control them. A GPS surveyor can then find himself or herself in the uncomfortable position of distorting a sound network of GPS positions to accommodate less accurate published coordinates.

Fortunately, GPS surveyors have a chance to contribute to the solution of these difficulties. NGS will accept GPS survey data submitted in the correct format with proper supporting documentation. The process, known as *blue-booking*, requires strict adherence to NGS specifications. GPS measurements that can meet the criteria are processed, classified, and incorporated into the NGRS for the benefit all GPS surveyors.

Other significant work along this line is underway in the state-by-state supernet programs. *High Accuracy Reference Networks (HARN)* are cooperative ventures between NGS and the states, and often include other organizations as well. With heavy reliance on GPS observations, these networks are intended to provide extremely accurate, vehicle-accessible, regularly spaced control points with good overhead visibility. To ensure coherence, when the GPS measurements are complete, they are submitted to NGS for inclusion in a statewide readjustment of the existing NGRS covered by the state. Coordinate shifts of 0.3 to 1.0 m from NAD83 values have been typical in these readjustments.

The most important aspect of HARNs is the accuracy of their final positions. Entirely new orders of accuracy have been developed for GPS relative positioning techniques by the *Federal Geodetic Control Committee (FGCC)*. The FGCC is an organization chartered in 1968 and composed of representatives from 11 agencies of the federal government. It revises and updates surveying standards for geodetic control networks, among other duties. Its provisional standards and specifications for GPS work include Orders AA, A, and B, which are defined as having minimum geometric accuracies of 3 mm ± 0.01 ppm, 5 mm ± 0.1 ppm, and 8 mm ± 1 ppm, respectively, at the 95 percent, or 2σ, confidence level. The adjusted positions of HARN stations are designed to provide statewide coverage of at least B Order control as set out in these new standards.

The publication of up-to-date geodetic data, always one of the most important functions of NGS, is even more crucial today. The format of the data published by NGS has changed somewhat. NAD83 information includes, of course, the new ellipsoidal latitudes, longitudes, and azimuths. However, unlike the NAD27 data that provided the elevations of only some control points, NAD83 data includes elevations, or heights, for all marked stations.

NAD83 Positions and Plane Coordinates

The newly published data also include state plane coordinates in the appropriate zone. As before, the easting and northing are accompanied by the mapping angle and grid azimuths, but a scale factor is also included for easy conversions. *Universal Transverse Mercator (UTM)* coordinates are among the new elements offered by NGS in the published information for NAD83 stations.

These plane coordinates, both state plane and UTM, are far from an anachronism. The UTM projection has been adopted by the IUGG, the same organization that reached the international agreement to use GRS80 as the reference ellipsoid for the modern geocentric datum. NATO and other military and civilian organizations worldwide also use UTM coordinates for various mapping needs. UTM coordinates are often useful to those planning work that embraces large areas. In the United States, state plane systems based on the transverse Mercator projection, an oblique Mercator projection, and the Lambert conic map projection, grid every state, Puerto Rico, and the U.S. Virgin Islands into their own plane rectangular coordinate system. And GPS surveys performed for local projects and mapping are frequently reported in the plane coordinates of one of these systems.

For states with large east-west extent, the Lambert conic projection is used. This system uses a projection cone that is imagined to intersect the ellipsoid at standard parallels. When the cone is *developed*; that is, opened to make a plane, the ellipsoidal meridians become straight lines that converge at the cone's apex. The apex is also the center of the circular lines that represent the projections of the parallels of latitude.

Some states use both the Lambert conic and the transverse Mercator projections for individual zones within the state system (Figures 5.7 and 5.8). Some rely on the transverse Mercator projection alone. The transverse Mercator projection uses a projection cylinder whose axis is imagined to be parallel to the earth's equator and perpendicular to its axis of rotation. It intersects the ellipsoid along standard lines parallel to a central meridian. However, after the cylinder is developed, all the projected meridians and parallels become curved lines.

Coordinates from these developed projections are given in reference to a Cartesian grid with two axes. Eastings are reckoned from an axis placed far west of the coordinate zone, adding a large constant value so all remain positive. Northings are reckoned from a line far to the south for the same reason.

The x-coordinate, the easting, and the y-coordinate, the northing, are expressed in either survey feet or international feet, depending on the state. NAD83 has required a redefinition of the state plane coordinate systems for the updated latitudes and longitudes. The constants now published by NGS are given in meters.

Both of these projections may be said to be *conformal*. Conformality means that an angle on the ellipsoid is preserved after mapping it onto the plane. This feature allows the shapes of small geographical features to look the same on the map as they do on the earth.

The UTM projection divides the world into 60 zones that begin at λ 180°, each with a width of 6° of longitude, extending from 84° Nϕ and 80° Sϕ. Its coverage is completed by the addition of two polar zones. The coterminus United States are within UTM zones 10 to 20.

The UTM grid is defined in meters. Each zone is projected onto a cylinder that is oriented in the same way as that used in the transverse Mercator state plane coordinates described above. The radius of the cylinder is chosen to keep the scale errors within acceptable limits. Coordi-

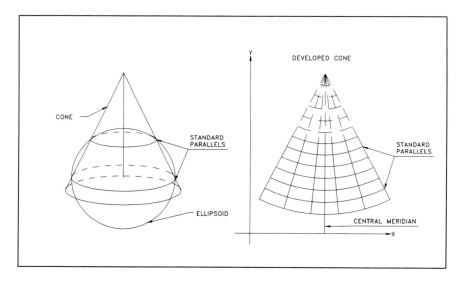

Figure 5.7. Lambert Conic Projection.

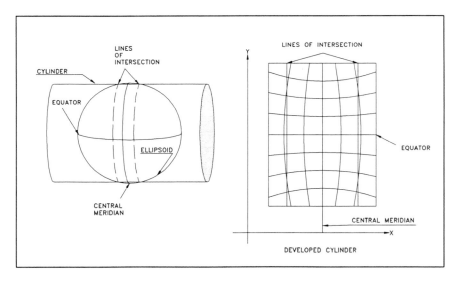

Figure 5.8. Transverse Mercator Projection.

nates of points from the reference ellipsoid within a particular zone are projected onto the UTM grid.

The intersection of each zone's central meridian with the equator defines its origin of coordinates. In the southern hemisphere, each origin is given the coordinates: easting $= X_0 = 500,000$ meters, and northing $= Y_0 =$

10,000,000 meters, to ensure that all points have positive coordinates. In the northern hemisphere, the values are: easting = X_0 = 500,000 meters, and northing = Y_0 = 0 meters, at the origin.

The scale factor grows from 0.9996 along the central meridian of a UTM zone to 1.00000 at 180,000 meters to the east and west. The state plane coordinate zones in the United States are limited to about 158 miles, and so embrace a smaller range of scale factors than do the UTM zones. In state plane coordinates, the variance in scale is usually no more than 1 part in 10,000. In UTM coordinates the variance can be as large as 1 part in 2,500.

The distortion of positions attributable to the transformation of NAD83 geodetic coordinates into the plane grid coordinates of any one of these projections is generally less than a centimeter. Most GPS and land surveying software packages provide routines for automatic transformation of latitude and longitude to and from these mapping projections. Similar programs can also be purchased from the NGS. Therefore, for most applications of GPS, there ought to be no technical compunction about expressing the results in grid coordinates. However, given the long traditions of plane surveying, it can be easy for some to lose sight of the geodetic context of the entire process that produced the final product of a GPS survey presented in plane coordinates.

The Deflection of the Vertical

Other new elements in the information published by NGS for NAD83 positions include deflection of the vertical. The deflection of the vertical can be defined as the angle made by a line perpendicular to the geoid that passes through a point on the earth's surface with a line that passes through the same point, but is perpendicular to the reference ellipsoid (Figure 5.9). Described another way, the deflection of the vertical is the angle between the direction of a plumb line with the ellipsoidal normal through the same point. The deflection of the vertical is usually broken down into two components, one in the plane of the meridian through the point and the other perpendicular to it. The first element is illustrated in Figure 5.9.

When surveyors relied on astronomical observations for the determination of latitude, longitude, and azimuth, calculation of the deflection of the vertical was critical to deriving the corresponding ellipsoidal coordinates from the work. Today, if the orientation of a GPS vector is checked with an astronomic azimuth, some discrepancy should be expected. The deflection of the vertical is a result of the irregularity of the geoid, and is mathematically related to separation between the geoid and the reference ellipsoid.

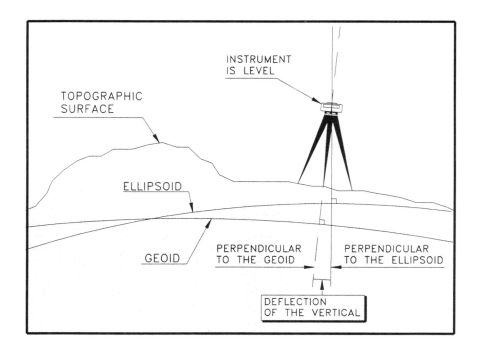

Figure 5.9. Deflection of the Vertical.

HEIGHTS

A point on the earth's surface is not completely defined by its latitude and longitude. In such a context there is, of course, a third element, that of height. Surveyors have traditionally referred to this component of a position as its elevation. One classical method of determining elevations is spirit leveling. As stated earlier, a level, correctly oriented at a point on the surface of the earth, defines a line parallel to the geoid at that point. Therefore, the elevations determined by level circuits are *orthometric;* that is, they are defined by their vertical distance above the geoid as it would be measured along a plumb line.

However, orthometric elevations are not directly available from the geocentric position vectors derived from GPS measurements. The vectors are not difficult to reduce to ellipsoidal latitude, longitude, and height because the reference ellipsoid is mathematically defined and clearly oriented to the earth. But the geoid defies such certain definition. As stated earlier, the geoid undulates with the uneven distribution of the mass of the earth, and has all the irregularity that implies. In fact, the separation between the bumpy surface of the geoid and the smooth GRS80 ellipsoid

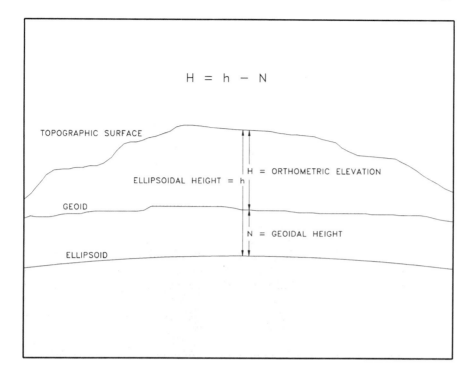

Figure 5.10. Formula for Transforming Ellipsoidal Heights.

varies from 0 up to ± 100 meters. Therefore, the only way a surveyor can convert an ellipsoidal height from a GPS observation on a particular station into a useable orthometric elevation is to know the extent of geoid-ellipsoid separation at that point.

Toward that end, major improvements have been made over the past quarter century or so in the mapping the geoid on both national and global scales. This work has gone a long way toward the accurate determination of the geoid-ellipsoid separation, known as *N*. The formula for transforming ellipsoidal heights, *h*, into orthometric elevations, *H*, is (Figure 5.10):

$$H = h - N$$

Chapter Six

Planning a Survey

ELEMENTS OF A GPS SURVEY DESIGN

If a GPS survey is carefully planned, it usually progresses smoothly. The technology has virtually conquered two stumbling blocks that have defeated the plans of conventional surveyors for generations. Inclement weather does not disrupt GPS observations, and a lack of intervisibility between stations is of no concern whatsoever. Still, GPS is far from so independent of conditions in the sky and on the ground that the process of designing a survey can now be reduced to points-per-day formulas, as some would like. Even with falling costs, the initial investment in GPS remains large by most surveyor's standards. However, there is seldom anything more expensive in a GPS project than a surprise.

How Much Planning Is Required?

New Standards

The Federal Geodetic Control Committee (FGCC) has written provisional accuracy standards for GPS relative positioning techniques. The older standards of first, second, and third order are classified under the rubric C in the new scheme. In the past, the cost of achieving first-order accuracy was considered beyond the reach of most conventional surveyors. Besides, surveyors often said that such results were far in excess of their needs, anyway. The burden of the equipment, techniques, and planning that is required to reach its 2σ relative error ratio of 1 part in 100,000 was something most surveyors were happy to leave to government agencies. But the FGCC's proposed new standards of B, A, and AA are, respectively, 10, 100 and 1000 times more accurate than the old first-order. The attainment of these accuracies does not require corresponding 10-, 100- and 1000-fold increases in equipment, training, personnel, or effort. They are now well within the reach of private GPS surveyors both economically and technically.

New Design Criteria

These upgrades in accuracy standards not only accommodate GPS, they also have cast survey design into a new light for many surveyors. Nevertheless, it is not correct to say that every job suddenly requires the highest achievable accuracy, nor is it correct to say that every GPS survey now demands an elaborate design. In some situations, a crew of two, or even one, surveyor onsite may carry a GPS survey from start to finish with no more of a plan than minute-to-minute decisions can provide, even though the basis and the content of those decisions may be quite different from those made in a conventional survey.

In areas that are not heavily treed and generally free of overhead obstructions, the now-lower C orders of accuracy may be possible without a prior design of any significance. But while it is certainly unlikely that a survey of photocontrol or work on a cleared construction site would present overhead obstructions problems comparable with a control survey in the Rocky Mountains, even such open work may demand preliminary attention. The location of vertical and horizontal control, access across privately owned property or government installations, or, if kinematic GPS is involved, the routes between the stations frequently require reconnaissance.

Still, there is an approach to kinematic and pseudokinematic GPS that tends to minimizes such concerns.

Radial GPS

Radial GPS surveying calls for one receiver, the base or foothold, to remain on a control station throughout the work while one or more other rover receivers move from point to point (Figure 6.1). The advantages of

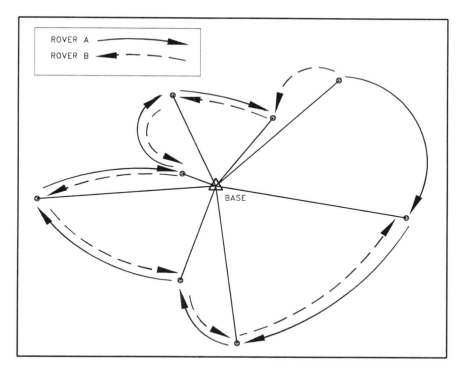

Figure 6.1. Radial GPS.

this arrangement in the stop-and-go kinematic or pseudokinematic modes include the large number of positions that can be established in a short amount of time with little or no planning. However, since all the baselines so established must originate at the base station, redundancy requires repeat occupations by the rovers with the same or different base control station. These successive occupations ought to be separated by at least a quarter of an hour and less than a full day, so the satellite constellation can reach a significantly different configuration. Further, lacking a preliminary design of the survey, the area must be free of overhead obstructions and sources of multipath. Project points that are simultaneously near one another but far from the control station must be directly connected with a baseline to maintain the integrity of the survey. Finally, if the base receiver loses lock and it goes unnoticed, it will completely defeat the radial survey.

Some of the difficulties of the radial survey approach can be overcome by adding more base control station receivers. More efficiency can be achieved by adding additional roving receivers. However, as the number of receivers rises, the logistics become more complicated, and a survey plan becomes necessary. In other words, in large GPS projects, in projects where overhead obstructions are a factor, or where ties to the National Geodetic Reference System are important, some level of reconnaissance and design is required. If the survey crew is new to GPS or the higher orders accuracy are called for, a survey design is certainly necessary.

Combining GPS Techniques

While kinematic and pseudokinematic techniques are well suited to radial surveys for some topographic, photogrammetric, and GIS work, static and rapid-static are generally more appropriate for control surveys. The most efficient application of GPS to a particular project may very well be a combination of all these techniques, and each may require a different level of planning. Nevertheless, it is static and rapid-static GPS that requires the fullest preliminary concern. The procedures presented here will be focused on the needs of that facet of GPS. While every element may not be necessary to a particular project or technique, it is very likely that some of them will.

Visiting the Site

Informing the Client

A visit to the site of a survey can often include a conference with the client. Particularly when the client is new to the technology, agreement on the cost and delivery date of a GPS project should be part of a larger body of information. GPS's reputation for extraordinary speed and accuracy can mislead some to expect miraculous, and impossible, results.

Even a small amount of understanding of the GPS surveying process goes a long way. For example, since the 3D Cartesian coordinates of GPS positions can be transformed into nearly any coherent coordinate system, a client may choose the form that is most useful to him or her. However, a mere list of coordinates may not be an adequate final product. The client may wish to have some formal account of the process that preceded the coordinates. A discussion of that report at the beginning of a project may save all concerned from subsequent misunderstandings.

The Lay of the Land

An initial visit to the site of the survey is not always possible, but it is almost always desirable. Although preliminary reconnaissance will certainly be cursory, general impressions may be formed on important questions that can be addressed more specifically later. For example, topography as it affects the line of sight between stations is of no concern on a GPS project, but its influence on transportation from station to station is a primary consideration in designing the survey. Perhaps some areas are only accessible by helicopter or other special vehicle. Initial inquiries can be made. Roads may be excellent in one area of the project and poor in another. The general density of vegetation, buildings, or fences may open general questions of overhead obstruction or multipath. The pattern of land ownership, relative to the location of project points, may raise or lower the level of concern about obtaining permission to cross property. Despite record information, the actual availability of horizontal and vertical control may be clearer on the ground of the project itself.

If night work, observations on or near highways, or unusual circumstances of any kind that may arouse public curiosity are anticipated, a visit with local law enforcement may be a good idea. Explanations at the earliest stages of a project can often eliminate difficulty later. The initial visit is also a good opportunity to learn about special safety regulations or other ordinances that will need to be satisfied during the project.

Client Participation

These and many more questions will arise, and certain answers will probably be few. It is not uncommon that the client is more familiar with the area than the surveyor, and can be a valuable resource in resolving many concerns. In fact, it is sometimes mutually convenient for the client to provide permissions, special vehicles, project point locations, or perform other tasks as part of the contractual arrangements.

Project Planning, Offsite

Maps

Maps are particularly valuable resources for preparing a GPS survey design. Local government and private sources can sometimes provide the most appropriate mapping. Depending on the scope of the survey, various scales and types of maps can be useful, but the standard for planning GPS surveys remains the USGS 7½- and 15-minute quad sheets.

A GPS survey plan usually begins in earnest with the plotting of all potential control and project points on a scale map of the area. USGS topographic maps from 1:24,000, the 7½ minute quadrangle, to 1:62,500, the 15-minute quadrangle, to maps at 1:250,000 scale provide a good foundation for this preparation. The location of roads, vegetation, boundaries, power lines, landing areas, and a wide variety of pertinent information is available immediately from these maps.

Other mapping that may be helpful is available from various government agencies: for example, the U.S. Forest Service in the Department of Agriculture; the Department of Interior's Bureau of Land Management, Bureau of Reclamation, and National Park Service; the U.S. Fish and Wildlife Service in the Department of Commerce; and the Federal Highway Administration in the Department of Transportation are just a few of them. Even county and city maps should be considered, since they can sometimes provide the most timely information available. However, one vital element of the design is not available from any of these maps: the NGRS stations.

NGS Control Data Sheets

It is quite important that to order the most up-to-date control information from NGS. The range of latitudes and longitudes defining the region of the survey is sufficient definition for the appropriate control quadrangle. It is best to ask for all the horizontal and vertical information within a region that is somewhat larger than that which is contained by the boundaries of the survey. The information is available in hard copy, in digital form on diskettes, or in the newest format covering some regions, CD-ROM. Control information is essential, but it can take some time to reach you. Therefore, it is best to order it at the earliest opportunity.

The information available from an NGS control sheet is valuable at the earliest stage of a GPS survey. See Figure 6.2 a, b, and c. In addition to the latitude and longitude, the published data include the state plane coordinates in the appropriate zones. The coordinates facilitate the plotting of the station's position on the project map.

New information available on NAD83 control sheets include UTM coordinates, geoidal heights, and deflection components. However, among the most useful new data for GPS survey planning is the name of the USGS quad where the particular station may be found. NGS control information is organized by NGS quads. The boundaries of these control quads do not correspond with those of the USGS quads. Correlating the location of an NGS control station with the appropriate USGS quad is made much easier by this addition.

Significance of the Information

The application of other information found on an NGS control sheet may not be as obvious. For example, the instrument height above the station mark is quite useful. If it is large, the implication is that a tower was

U.S. DEPARTMENT OF COMMERCE
NATIONAL OCEANIC AND ATMOSPHERIC ADMINISTRATION
NATIONAL OCEAN SURVEY
ROCKVILLE, MARYLAND 20852
NOAA FORM 76-107(5-72)
DATE JAN 1978

ALPHABETICAL INDEX TO
HORIZONTAL CONTROL DATA
by the
National Ocean Survey

PAGE 1
QUADS 421241-2-3-4 & 431241-2-3-4
ORE
LATITUDE 42°00' TO 44°00'
LONGITUDE 124°00' TO 125°00'
DIAGRAM NK 10-1,4 COOS BAY

STATION NAME	QUAD NO.	STATION NO.	KEY NO.
ACORN	1871	421242	1001
ADAMS	1942	431241	1001
ALDER USE	1920	431241	1002
ANDERSON USGS	1942	431242	1001
APPLE	1928	431241	1003
APRIL	1928	431241	1004
ARAGO	1922	431242	1002
ARAGO HEAD USGS	1945	431242	1003
ARAGO PEAK USGS	1945	431242	1004
ARAGO PEAK 2	1945	431242	1005
ARCH ROCK	1869	421244	1001
ARMY	1920	431241	LOST
ARMY HILL	1885	431241	1005
AT	1920	431241	1006
AZALEA ORHD	1937	431242	1006

STATION NAME	QUAD NO.	STATION NO.	KEY NO.
BENCH MARK 23 USGS	1965	431242	1014
BENCH MARK D 249 ORHD	1965	431242	1015
BENCH MARK S 198 ORHD	1956	431241	1012
BENCH MARK V 197 ORHD	1965	431242	1016
BEND USE	1937	431242	1017
BEND 2 USE	1937	431242	1018
BENN	1942	421241	1005
BENNETT	1906	421241	1006
BENNETT LOOKOUT TOWER	1942	421241	1007
BERNHART	1956	431241	1013
BEST ROCK	1869	421244	1002
BILL	1920	431241	1014
BILL	1907	431242	1019
BILL BUTTE LOOKOUT TOWER	1942	431242	1021
BILL RESET USGS	1942	431242	1020

Figure 6.2(a). Format of the NGS Index of Horizontal Control Data.

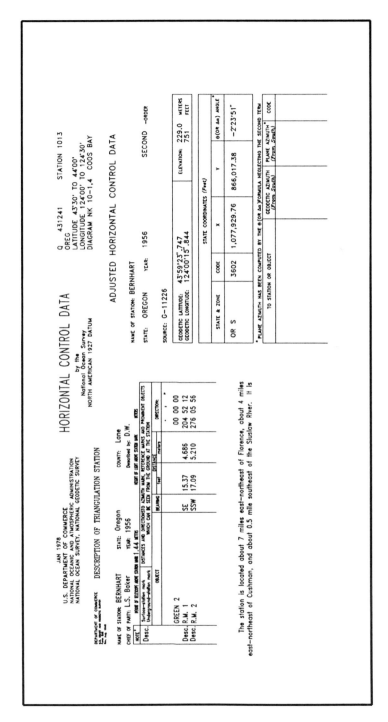

Figure 6.2(b). Format of the Old NGS Horizontal Control Data Sheet.

```
SU1075   National Geodetic Survey,        Retrieval Date = July 20, 1993
SU1075   * * * * * * * * * * * * * * * * * * * * * * * * * * * * * * * * * *
SU1075   DESIGNATION    -   7 RHM
SU1075   PID            -   SU1075
SU1075   STATE/COUNTY   -   MT/FLATHEAD
SU1075   USGS QUAD      -   BEND
SU1075
SU1075   HORZ DATUM     -   NAD 83
SU1075   VERT DATUM     -   NAVD 88
SU1075
SU1075   POSITION       -   47 52 39.        (N)   115 00 48.       (W)    SCALED
SU1075   83 minus 27    -          -00                     +04                   NADCON
SU1075
SU1075   HEIGHT         -        987.886   (meters)   3241.09   (feet)    ADJUST
SU1075   88 MINUS 29    -          +1.20                                        UNADJ DIF
SU1075   * * * * * * * * * * * * * * * * * * * * * * * * * * * * * * * * * *
SU1075   GEOID HEIGHT   -        -15.88
SU1075   MODELED GRAV   -   980,540.2
SU1075   VERT ORDER     -   THIRD     CLASS 0
```

Figure 6.2(c). Format of the New Control Data—Benchmark.

used in the original observations from the station. Such a station might lack the necessary overhead visibility for a GPS observation.

The value of the description of the monument's location and the route used to reach it is directly proportional to the date it was prepared and the remoteness of its location. The conditions around older stations often change dramatically when the area has become accessible to the public. If the age and location of a station increases the probability that it has been disturbed or destroyed, then reference monuments can be noted as alternatives worthy of onsite investigation. However, special care ought to be taken to ensure that the reference monuments are not confused with the station marks themselves.

Horizontal Control

At this stage, the choice of horizontal control amounts to finding candidates for actual reconnaissance. Excepting work tied to High Accuracy Reference Network (HARN) control, the so-called *supernet stations*, the accuracy of GPS measurements frequently exceed that of the stations used to control them. Since the final network of a GPS survey may well require constraint to NGS stations of somewhat inferior accuracy, those with the highest-available order should always be preferred. However, these provisional decisions about horizontal control require consideration of more than the published accuracy of the stations.

When geodetic surveying was more dependent on optics than electronic signals from space, horizontal control stations were set with station intervisibility in mind, not ease of access. Therefore it is not surprising that they are frequently difficult to reach. Not only are they found on the tops of buildings and mountains, they are also in woods, beside transmission towers, near fences, and generally obstructed from GPS signals. The geodetic surveyors that established them could hardly have foreseen a time when a clear view of the sky above their heads would be crucial to high-quality control.

In fact, it is only recently that most private surveyors have had any routine use for NGS stations. Many station marks have not been occupied for quite a long time. Since the primary monuments are often found deteriorated, overgrown, unstable, or destroyed, it is important that surveyors be well acquainted with the underground marks, reference marks, and other methods used to perpetuate control stations.

Obviously, it is a good idea to propose reconnaissance of several more than the absolute minimum of three horizontal control stations. Fewer than three makes any check of their positions virtually impossible. Many more are usually required in a GPS route survey. In general, in GPS networks the more well-chosen horizontal control stations that are available, the better. Some stations will almost certainly prove unsuitable unless they have been used previously in GPS work or are part of a HARN.

Station Location

The location of the stations, relative to the GPS project itself, is also an important consideration in choosing horizontal control. For work other than route surveys, a handy rule of thumb is to divide the project into four quadrants and to choose at least one horizontal control station in each. The actual survey should have at least one horizontal control station in three of the four quadrants. Each of them ought to be as near as possible to the project boundary. Supplementary control in the interior of the network can then be used to add more stability to the network (Figure 6.3).

At a minimum, route surveys require horizontal control at the beginning, the end, and the middle. Long routes should be bridged with control on both sides of the line at appropriate intervals. The standard symbol for indicating horizontal control on the project map is a triangle.

Vertical Control

Some NAD27 stations and all NAD83 stations have published orthometric elevations. Those stations with a published accuracy high enough for consideration as vertical control are symbolized by an open square or circle on the map. Those stations that are sufficient for both horizontal and vertical control are particularly helpful and are designated by a combination of the triangle and square (or circle).

A minimum of four vertical control stations is needed to anchor a GPS network. A large project should have more. In general, the more high-order benchmarks that are available, the better. Vertical control is best located at the four corners of a project.

Orthometric elevations are best transferred by means of classic spirit leveling. When vertical control is too far removed from the project or when the benchmarks are obstructed, if project efficiency is not drastically impaired, such work should be built into the project plan. When the distances involved are too long, two independent GPS measurements may suffice to connect a benchmark to the project. However, it is important to recall the difference between the ellipsoidal heights available from a GPS observation and the orthometric elevations yielded by a level circuit. Further, third-

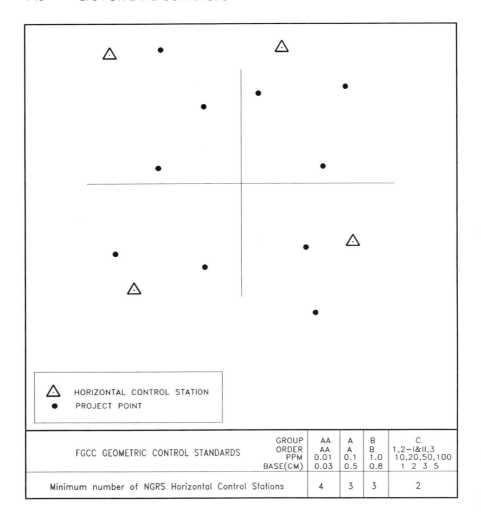

FGCC GEOMETRIC CONTROL STANDARDS	GROUP	AA	A	B	C
	ORDER	AA	A	B	1,2-I&II,3
	PPM	0.01	0.1	1.0	10,20,50,100
	BASE(CM)	0.03	0.5	0.8	1 2 3 5
Minimum number of NGRS Horizontal Control Stations		4	3	3	2

Figure 6.3. Horizontal Control and Project Points.

order level work is not improved by beginning at a first-order benchmark. When spirit levels are planned to provide vertical control positions, special care may be necessary to ensure that the precision of the conventional work is as consistent as possible with the rest of the GPS survey (Figure 6.4).

Route surveys require vertical control at the beginning and the end. They should be bridged with benchmarks on both sides of the line at intervals from 5 to 10 km.

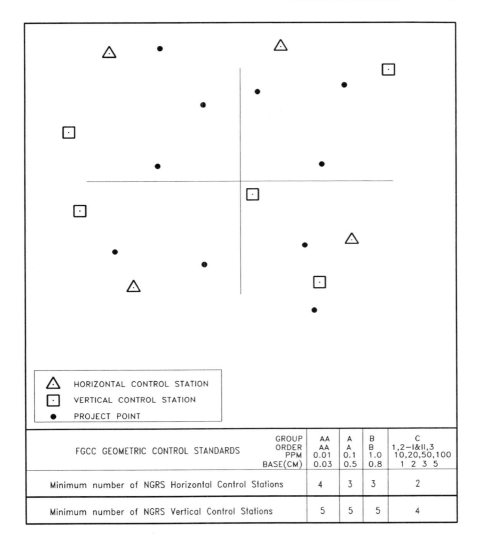

FGCC GEOMETRIC CONTROL STANDARDS	GROUP ORDER PPM BASE(CM)	AA AA 0.01 0.03	A A 0.1 0.5	B B 1.0 0.8	C 1,2–I&II,3 10,20,50,100 1 2 3 5
Minimum number of NGRS Horizontal Control Stations		4	3	3	2
Minimum number of NGRS Vertical Control Stations		5	5	5	4

Figure 6.4. Horizontal Control, Vertical Control and Project Points.

Plotting Project Points

A solid dot is the standard symbol used to indicate the position of project points. Some variation is used when a distinction must be drawn between those points that are in place and those that must be set. When its location is appropriate, it is always a good idea to have a vertical or horizontal control station serve double duty as a project point. While the precision of their plotting may vary, it is important that project points be located as precisely as possible, even at this preliminary stage.

First, the accuracy of the approximate coordinates of the project points later scaled from the map often depend on their original plotting. These approximate coordinates will give the GPS receiver, which eventually occupies the point, a reference position to begin its acquisition of satellites during the actual observation. The more accurate the reference's position, the faster the satellites can be acquired. Second, the subsequent observation schedule will depend to some degree on the arrangement of the baselines drawn on the map to connect the plotted points. Third, the preliminary evaluation of access, obstructions, and other information that can be derived from the map depends on the position of the project point relative to these features.

Evaluating Access

When all potential control and project positions have been plotted on the map and given a unique identifier, some aspects of the survey can be addressed a bit more specifically. If good roads are favorably located, if open areas are indicated around the stations, and if no station falls in an area where special permission will be required for its occupation, then the preliminary plan of the survey ought to be remarkably trouble-free. However, it is likely that one or more of these conditions will not be so fortunately arranged.

The speed and efficiency of transportation from station to station can be assessed to some degree from the project map. It is also wise to remember that while inclement weather does not disturb GPS observations whatsoever, without sufficient preparation it can play havoc with the surveyor's ability to reach points over difficult roads or by aircraft.

In the case of a plan of survey for kinematic GPS, the route between the stations must be carefully examined onsite for any indication of overhead obstructions that may cause the receiver to lose lock en route. The most likely course can only be marked for reconnaissance at this stage. Features to avoid include trees, tunnels, bridges that cross over a road, and tall buildings that are near the road. A strategy where loss of lock is unavoidable is to set control on both sides of the obstruction so the receiver can be reinitialized.

Planning Offsets

If control stations or project points are located in areas where the map indicates that topography or vegetation will obstruct the satellite's signals, alternatives may be considered. A shift of the position of a project point into a clear area may be possible where the change does not have a significant effect on the overall network. A control station may also be the basis for a less obstructed position, transferred with a short level circuit or traverse. Of course, such a transfer requires availability of conventional surveying equipment on the project (which will be covered later). In situations where such movement is not possible, careful consideration of the actual paths of the satellites at the station itself during onsite reconnaissance may reveal enough windows in the gaps between obstructions to collect sufficient data by strictly defining the observation sessions (which will be discussed later, also).

Planning Azimuth Marks

Azimuth marks are a common requirement in GPS projects. They are almost always a necessary accompaniment to GPS stations when a client intends to use them to control subsequent conventional surveying work. Of course, the line between the station and the azimuth mark should be as long as convenience and the preservation of line-of-sight allows.

It is wise to take care that short baselines do not degrade the overall integrity of the project. Occupations of the station and its azimuth mark should be simultaneous for a direct measurement of the baseline between them. Both should also be tied to the larger network as independent stations. There should be two or more occupations of each station when the distance between them is less than 2 km.

While an alternative approach may be to derive the azimuth between a GPS station and its azimuth mark with an astronomic observation, it is important to remember that a small error, attributable to the deflection of the vertical, will be present in such an observation. The small angle between the plumb line and a normal to the ellipsoid at the station can either be ignored or removed with a LaPlace correction.

Obtaining Permissions

Another aspect of access can be considered when the project map finally shows all the pertinent points. Nothing can bring a well-planned survey to a halt faster than a locked gate, an irate landowner, or a government official who is convinced he should have been consulted, previously. To the extent that it is possible from the available mapping, affected private landowners and government jurisdictions should be identified and contacted. Taking this precaution at the earliest stage of the survey planning can increase the chance that the sometimes long process of obtaining permissions, gate keys, badges, or other credentials has a better chance of completion before the survey begins.

Any aspect of a GPS survey plan derived from examining maps must be considered preliminary. Most features change with time, and even those that are relatively constant cannot be portrayed on a map with complete exactitude. Nevertheless, steps toward a coherent workable design can be taken using the information they provide.

Some GPS Survey Design Facts

Though much of the preliminary work in producing the plan of a GPS survey is a matter of estimation, some hard facts must be considered, too. For example, the number of GPS receivers available for the work and the number of satellites above the observer's horizon at a given time in a given place are two ingredients that can be determined with some certainty.

Software Assistance

Most GPS software packages provide users with routines that help them determine the satellite *windows*, the periods of time when the largest number of satellites are simultaneously available. Now that the GPS system is operational and a full constellation of Block I and II satellites are in orbit, observers are virtually assured of 24-hour, four-satellite coverage. This assurance is a welcome relief from the forced downtime in the early days of GPS. The delays that were caused by periods when the satellites in view numbered three and fewer are now virtually eliminated. However, the mere presence of four satellites above an observer's horizon does not guarantee collection of sufficient data. Therefore, despite the virtual certainty that at least four satellites will be available, evaluation of their configuration as expressed in the position dilution of precision (PDOP) is still crucial in planning a GPS survey.

PDOP

In GPS, the receiver's position is derived from the simultaneous solution of vectors between it and at least four satellites. The quality of that solution depends, in large part, on the distribution of the vectors. For example, any position determined when the satellites are crowded together in one part of the sky will be unreliable, because all the vectors will have virtually the same direction. Given the ephemeris of each satellite, the approximate position of the receiver, and the time of the planned observation, a computer can predict such an unfavorable configuration and indicate the problem by giving the PDOP a large number. The GPS survey planner, on notice that the PDOP is large for a particular period of time, should consider an alternate observation plan.

On the other hand, when one satellite is directly above the receiver and three others are near the horizon and 120° in azimuth from one another, the arrangement is nearly ideal for a four-satellite constellation. The planner of the survey would be likely to consider such a window. However, more satellites would improve the resulting position even more, as long as they are well distributed in the sky above the receiver. In general, the more satellites, the better. For example, if the planner finds eight satellites will be above the horizon in the region where the work is to be done and the PDOP is below 2, that window would be a likely candidate for observation.

There are other important considerations. The satellites are constantly moving in relation to the receiver and to each other. Satellites rise and set, and the PDOP is constantly changing. Within all this movement, the GPS survey designer must have some way of correlating the longest and most important baselines with the longest windows, the most satellites, and the lowest PDOP. Most GPS software packages, given a particular location and period of time, can provide illustrations of the satellite configuration.

Polar Plot

One such diagram is a plot of the satellite's tracks drawn on a graphical representation of the upper half of the celestial sphere, with the observer's zenith at the center and perimeter circle as the horizon. The azimuths and elevations of the satellites above the specified mask angle are connected into arcs that represent the paths of all available satellites. The utility of this sort of drawing has lessened with the completion of the GPS constellation. In fact, there are so many satellites available that the picture can become quite crowded and difficult to decipher.

Another printout is a tabular list of the elevation and azimuth of each satellite at time intervals selected by the user.

An Example

The position of point Morant in the Table 6.1 needed expression to the nearest minute only, a sufficient approximation for the purpose. The ephem-

Table 6.1. Azimuth and Elevation Table

Satellites
Azimuth and Elevation Table

Point: Morant
Date: Wed., Sept. 29, 1993
24 Satellites: 1 2 3 7 9 12 13 14 15 16 17 18 19 20 21 22 23 24 25 26 27 28 29 31
Sampling Rate: 10 minutes

Lat 36:45:0 N   Lon 121:45:0W   Ephemeris: 9/24/93
Mask Angle: 15 (deg)   Time Zone: Pacific Day (−7)

Time	El	Az	El	Az	El	Az	El	Az	El	Az	El	Az	El	Az	El	Az	PDOP
SV	2		16		18				27		28		29		31		*constellation of 8 SVs*
0:00	16	219	15	317	77	121			66	330	23	287	36	129	30	109	1.7
0:10	20	221	18	314	73	131			67	341	22	292	32	132	33	104	1.8
0:20	24	223	20	310	68	137			68	353	21	297	28	135	35	99	1.8
0:30	28	226	22	306	64	142			68	5	20	302	24	138	36	93	1.9
0:40	32	229	23	302	59	146			67	17	18	308	20	140	37	88	1.8
0:50	36	232	24	297	54	148			66	28	16	314	16	142	38	82	1.8
SV	2		16		18				27		28		29				*constellation of 6 SVs*
1:00	40	235	24	293	49	151			65	39	58	320	38	76			3.0
1:10	43	239	24	288	44	153			63	49	61	328	37	70			3.0
1:20	47	244	24	283	40	155			61	57	64	336	36	64			2.8
1:30	51	249	23	278	35	156			59	65	66	345	34	60			2.6
SV	2		7		16		18		19		27				31		*constellation of 7 SVs*
1:40	54	254	16	186	22	273	30	157	56	73	68	356			32	55	2.3
1:50	57	260	21	186	20	269	26	158	53	79	70	9			29	51	2.2
2:00	60	268	25	186	19	264	22	159	50	85	71	23			26	48	2.0
SV	2		7		16		18		19		27		29		31		*constellation of 8 SVs*
2:10	66	276	30	185	16	260	17	160	47	91	15	319	71	38	23	45	1.7

eris data were 5 days old when the chart was generated by the computer, but the data were still an adequate representation of the satellite's movements to use in planning. The mask angle was specified at 15°, so the program would consider a satellite set when it moved below that elevation angle. The zone time was Pacific Daylight Time, 7 hours behind Coordinated Universal Time, UTC. The full constellation provided 24 healthy satellites, and the sampling rate indicated that the azimuth and elevation of those above the mask angle would be shown every 10 minutes.

At 0:00 hour satellite PRN 2 could be found on an azimuth of 219° and an elevation of 16° above the horizon by an observer at 36°45'Nϕ and 121°45'Wλ. The table indicates that PRN 2 was rising, and got continually higher in the sky for the 2 hours and 10 minutes covered by the chart. The satellite PRN 16 was also rising at 0:00, but reached its maximum altitude at about 1:10 and began to set. Unlike PRN 2, PRN 16 was not tabulated in the same row throughout the chart. It was supplanted when PRN 7 rose above the mask angle and PRN 16 shifted one column to the right. The same may be said of PRN 18 and PRN 19. Both of these satellites began high in the sky, unlike PRN 28 and PRN 29. They were just above 15° and setting when the table began and set after approximately 1 hour of availability. They would not have been seen again at this location for about 12 hours.

This chart indicated changes in the available constellation from eight space vehicles, *SVs*, between 0:00 and 0:50, six between 1:00 and 1:30, seven from 1:40 to 2:00, and back to eight at 2:10. The constellation never dipped below the minimum of four satellites, and the PDOP was good throughout. The PDOP varied between a low of 1.7 and a high of 3.0. Over the interval covered by the table, the PDOP never reached the unsatisfactory level of 5 or 6, which is when a planner should avoid observation.

Choosing the Window

Using this chart, the GPS survey designer might well have concluded that the best available window was the first. There was nearly an hour of eight-satellite data with a PDOP below 2. However, the data indicated that good observations could be made at any time covered here, except for one thing: it was the middle of the night. When a small number of satellites were available in the early days of GPS, the discomfort of such observations were ignored from necessity. With a full constellation, the loss of sleep can be avoided, and the designer may look at a more convenient time of day to begin the field work.

Ionospheric Delay

It is worth noting that the ionospheric refraction error is usually smaller after sundown. In fact, the FGCC specifies two-frequency receivers for daylight observations that hope to meet AA-, A-, and B-order accuracy standards, due, in part, to the increased ionospheric delay during those hours. There are provisions for compensation by modeling the error with two-frequency data from other sources where only single-frequency receivers are available. However, the specification illustrates the importance of considering atmospheric error sources.

An Example

Table 6.2, later in the day, covers a period of two hours when a constellation of five and six satellites was always available. However, through the first hour, from 6:30 to 7:30, the PDOP hovered around 5 and 6. For the first half of that hour, four of the satellites—PRN 9, PRN 12, PRN 13, and PRN 24—were all near the same elevation. During the same period, PRN 9 and PRN 12 were only approximately 50° apart in azimuth, as well. Even though a sufficient constellation of satellites was constantly available, the survey designer may well have considered only the last 30 to 50 minutes of the time covered by this chart as suitable for observation.

There is one caution, however. Azimuth-elevation tables are a convenient tool in the division of the observing day into sessions, but it should not be taken for granted that every satellite listed is healthy and in service. For the actual availability of satellites and an update on atmospheric conditions, it is always wise to call the recorded message on the United States Coast Guard hotline at (703) 313-5907 or the computer bulletin board at (703) 313-5910 before and after a project. In the planning stage, the call can prevent creation of a design dependent on satellites that prove unavailable. Similarly, after the field work is completed, it can prevent inclusion of unhealthy data in the postprocessing.

Supposing that the period from 7:40 to 8:30 was found to be a good window, the planner may have regarded it as a single 50-minute session, or divided it into shorter sessions. One aspect of that decision was probably the length of the baseline in question. In static GPS, a long line of 30 km may require 50 minutes of six-satellite data, but a short line of 3 km may not. If the planned survey was not done by static GPS, but instead with rapid-static, a 10-minute session may have been sufficient—in kinematic work the required session may be even shorter. Therefore, another aspect of the decision as to how the window was divided probably depended on the anticipated GPS surveying technique. A third consideration was prob-

Table 6.2. Azimuth and Elevation Table Later in the Day

Satellites

Azimuth and Elevation Table

Point: Morant
Date: Wed., Sept. 29, 1993   Lat 36:45:0 N   Lon 121:45:0W   Mask Angle: 15 (deg)   Ephemeris: 9/24/93   Time Zone: Pacific Day (−7)
24 Satellites: 1 2 3 7 9 12 13 14 15 16 17 18 19 20 21 22 23 24 25 26 27 28 29 31
Sampling Rate: 10 minutes

Time	El	Az	El	Az	El	Az	El	Az	El	Az	El	Az	El	Az	PDOP
SV	7		9		12		13						24		
							constellation of 5 SVs								
6:30	28	54	60	271	61	319	62	15					48	177	6.3
6:40	24	57	60	261	66	314	57	19					53	176	6.0
6:50	21	60	59	252	70	305	53	22					58	175	5.3
7:00	18	62	57	243	73	292	49	25					63	172	4.6
SV			9		12		13				20		24		
							constellation of 5 SVs								
7:10			54	235	74	274	44	28			16	308	68	169	4.8
7:20			51	229	74	255	40	32			20	310	72	163	5.7
7:30			47	224	72	238	37	35			23	311	77	153	5.1
7:40			43	219	68	226	33	38			27	313	80	134	4.0
SV			9		12		13		16		20		24		
							constellation of 6 SVs								
7:50			39	215	64	218	29	41	16	149	31	314	81	102	2.1
8:00			35	212	59	213	26	45	19	146	36	314	80	73	2.3
8:10			31	209	54	209	23	48	23	143	40	315	76	57	2.4
8:20			27	207	49	206	19	52	27	140	44	314	72	49	2.5
8:30			23	204	44	204	16	55	30	137	48	314	67	45	2.5

ably the approximation of the time necessary to move from one station to another. More about the length of the baselines and estimated transportation times later.

Naming the Variables

The next step in the GPS survey design is drawing the preliminary plan of the baselines on the project map. Once some idea of the configuration of the baselines has been established, an observation schedule can be organized. Toward that end, the FGCC has developed a set of formulas provided in Appendix F of their provisional *Geometric Geodetic Accuracy Standards and Specifications for Using GPS Relative Positioning Techniques*. Those formulas will be used here.

For illustration, suppose that the project map (Figure 6.5) includes horizontal control, vertical control, and project points for a planned GPS network. They will be symbolized by *m*. There are four dual-frequency GPS receivers available for this project. They will be symbolized by *r*. There will be five observation sessions each day during the project. They will be symbolized by *d*. To summarize:

m = total number of stations (existing and new) = 14
d = number of possible observing sessions per observing day = 5
r = number of receivers = 4 dual frequency

The design developed from this map must be preliminary. The session for each day of observation will depend on the success of the work the day before. Despite best efforts, any plan based on a map must be provisional until the baseline lengths, the obstructions at the observation sites, the transportation difficulties, the ionospheric disturbances, and the satellite geometry are actually known. Those questions can only be answered during the reconnaissance and the observations that follow. Even though these equivocations apply, the next step is to draw the baselines measurement plan.

Drawing the Baselines

Horizontal Control

A good rule of thumb is to verify the integrity of the horizontal control by observing baselines between these stations first. The vectors can be used to both corroborate the accuracy of the published coordinates, and

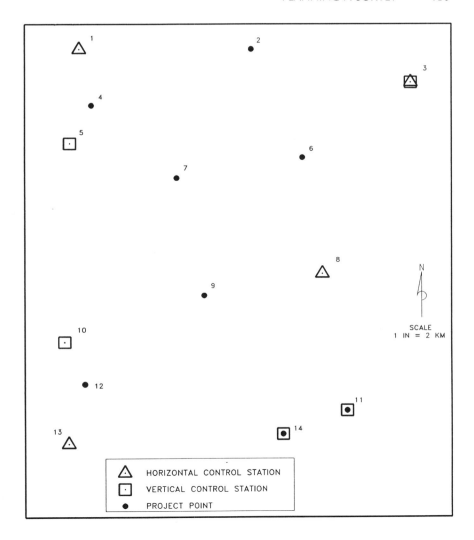

Figure 6.5. Project Map.

later to resolve the scale, shift, and rotation parameters between the control positions and the new network that will be determined by GPS.

These baselines are frequently the longest in the project, and there is an added benefit to measuring them first. By processing a portion of the data collected on the longest baselines early in the project, the degree that the sessions could have been shortened without degrading the quality of the measurement can be found. This test may allow improvement in the productivity on the job without erosion of the final positions (Figure 6.6).

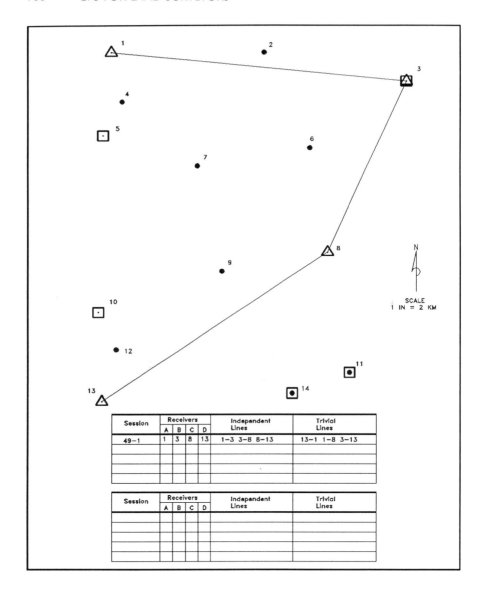

Figure 6.6. Drawing the Baselines.

Julian Day in Naming Sessions

The table at the bottom of Figure 6.6 indicates that the name of the first session connecting the horizontal control is 49-1. The date of the planned session is given in the Julian system. Taken most literally, Julian dates are counted from January 1, 4713 B.C. However, most practitioners of GPS use the term to mean the day of the current year measured consecutively from January 1. Under this construction, since there are 31 days in January, Julian day 49 is February 18 of the current year. The designation 49-1 means that this is to be the first session on that day. Some prefer to use letters to distinguish the session. In that case, the label would be 49-A.

Independent Lines

This project will be done with four receivers. The table shows that receiver A will occupy point 1; receiver B, point 3; receiver C, point 8; and receiver D, point 13 in the first session. However, the illustration shows only three of the possible six baselines that will be produced by this arrangement. Only the *independent*, also known as *nontrivial*, lines are shown on the map. The three lines that are not drawn are called *trivial*, and are also known as *dependent lines*. This idea is based on restricting the use of the lines created in each observing session to the absolute minimum needed to produce a unique solution.

Whenever four receivers are used, six lines are created. However, any three of those lines will fully define the position of each occupied station in relation to the others in the session. Therefore, the user can consider any three of the six lines independent, but once the decision is made, only those three baselines are included in the network. The remaining baselines are then considered trivial and discarded. In practice, the three shortest lines in a four-receiver session are almost always deemed the independent vectors, and the three longest lines are eliminated as trivial, or dependent. That is the case with the session illustrated.

Where r is the number of receivers, every session yields $r-1$ independent baselines. For example, four receivers used in 10 sessions would produce 30 independent baselines. It cannot be said that the shortest lines are always chosen to be the independent lines. Sometimes there are reasons to reject one of the shorter vectors due to incomplete data, cycle slips, multipath, or some other weakness in the measurements. Before such decisions can be made, each session will require analysis after the data have actually been collected. In the planning stage, it is best to consider the shortest vectors as the independent lines.

Another aspect of the distinction between independent and trivial lines involves the concept of error of closure. Any loop closures that only use baselines derived from a single common GPS session will yield an apparent error of zero, because they are derived from the same simultaneous observations. For example, all the baselines between the four receivers in session 49-1 of the illustrated project will be based on ranges to the same GPS satellites over the same period of time. Therefore, the trivial lines of 13-1, 1-8, and 3-13 will be derived from the same information used to determine the independent lines of 1-3, 3-8, and 8-13. It follows that, if the fourth line from station 13 to station 1 were included to close the figure of the illustrated session, the error of closure would be zero. The same may be said of the inclusion of any of the trivial lines. Their addition cannot add any redundancy or any geometric strength to the lines of the session, because they are all derived from the same data. If redundancy cannot be added to a GPS session by including any more than the minimum number of independent lines, how can the baselines be checked? Where does redundancy in GPS work come from?

Redundancy

If only two receivers were used to complete the illustrated project, there would be no trivial lines, and it might seem there would be no redundancy at all. But to connect every station with its closest neighbor, each station would have to be occupied at least twice, and each time during a different session. For example, with receiver A on station 1 and receiver B on station 2, the first session could establish the baseline between them. The second session could then be used to measure the baseline between station 1 and station 4. It would certainly be possible to simply move receiver B to station 4 and leave receiver A undisturbed on station 1. However, some redundancy could be added to the work if receiver A were reset. If it were recentered, replumbed, and its H.I. remeasured, some check on both of its occupations on station 1 would be possible when the network was completed. Under this scheme, a loop closure at the end of the project would have some meaning.

If one were to use such a scheme on the illustrated project and connect into one loop all of the 14 baselines determined by the 14 two-receiver sessions, the resulting error of closure would be useful. It could be used to detect blunders in the work, such as mis-measured H.I.s. Such a loop would include many different sessions. The ranges between the satellites and the receivers defining the baselines in such a circuit would be from different constellations at different times. On the other hand, if it were possible to occupy all 14 stations in the illustrated project with 14 different receivers simultaneously and do the entire survey in one session, a loop closure would be absolutely meaningless.

In the real world, such a project is not usually done with 14 receivers nor with 2 receivers, but with 3, 4, or 5. The achievement of redundancy takes a middle road. The number of independent occupations is still an important source of redundancy. In the two-receiver arrangement every line can be independent, but that is not the case when a project is done with any larger number of receivers. As soon as three or more receivers are considered, the discussion of redundant measurement must be restricted to independent baselines, excluding trivial lines.

Redundancy is then partly defined by the number of independent baselines that are measured more than once, as well as by the percentage of stations that are occupied more than once. While it is not possible to repeat a baseline without reoccupying its endpoints, it is possible to reoccupy a large percentage of the stations in a project without repeating a single baseline. These two aspects of redundancy in GPS—the repetition of independent baselines and the reoccupation of stations—are somewhat separate.

FGCC Standards for Redundancy

To meet order AA geometric accuracy standards, the FGCC requires three or more occupations on 80 percent of the stations in a project. Three or more occupations are necessary on 40, 20, and 10 percent of the stations for A, B, and C standards, respectively. When the distance between a station and its azimuth mark is less than 2 km, both points must be occupied at least twice to meet any standard above 2nd order. All vertical control stations must be occupied at least twice for all orders of accuracy. Two or more occupations are required for all horizontal control stations in order AA. The percentage requirements for repeat occupations on horizontal control stations drops to 75, 50, and 25 percent for A, B, and C, respectively. For new project points, reoccupation is mandated on 80, 50, and 10 percent of the stations in the project for A, B, and C, respectively.

The standards for repeat measurements of independent baselines in the FGCC provisional specifications note that an equal number of N-S and E-W vectors should be remeasured in a network. Of the independent baselines, 25 percent should be repeated in a project to meet order AA geometric accuracy standards. The standards require 15, 5, and 5 percent for orders A, B, and C, respectively.

Unless a project is to be *blue-booked*; that is, submitted to the NGS for inclusion in the national network, or there is a contractual obligation, there is usually no need to meet the letter of the specifications listed above. They are offered here as an indication of the level of redundancy that is necessary for high-accuracy GPS work.

Figure 6.7 shows one of the many possible approaches to setting up the baselines for this particular GPS project. The survey design calls for the horizontal control to be occupied in session 49-1. It is to be followed by measurements between two control stations and the nearest adjacent project

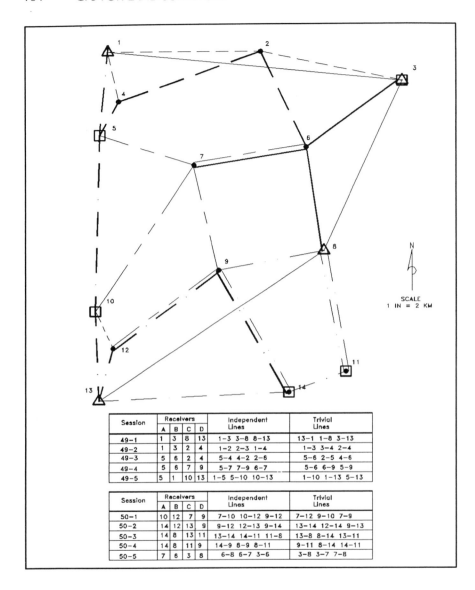

Session	Receivers				Independent Lines	Trivial Lines
	A	B	C	D		
49-1	1	3	8	13	1-3 3-8 8-13	13-1 1-8 3-13
49-2	1	3	2	4	1-2 2-3 1-4	1-3 3-4 2-4
49-3	5	6	2	4	5-4 4-2 2-6	5-6 2-5 4-6
49-4	5	6	7	9	5-7 7-9 6-7	5-6 6-9 5-9
49-5	5	1	10	13	1-5 5-10 10-13	1-10 1-13 5-13

Session	Receivers				Independent Lines	Trivial Lines
	A	B	C	D		
50-1	10	12	7	9	7-10 10-12 9-12	7-12 9-10 7-9
50-2	14	12	13	9	9-12 12-13 9-14	13-14 12-14 9-13
50-3	14	8	13	11	13-14 14-11 11-8	13-8 8-14 13-11
50-4	14	8	11	9	14-9 8-9 8-11	9-11 8-14 14-11
50-5	7	6	3	8	6-8 6-7 3-6	3-8 3-7 7-8

Figure 6.7. One Approach to Setting Baselines.

points in session 49-2. As shown in the table at the bottom of Figure 6.7, there will be redundant occupations on stations 1 and 3. Even though the same receivers will occupy those points, their operators will be instructed to reset them at different H.I.s for the new session. A better, but probably less efficient, plan would be to occupy these stations with different receivers than were used in the first session.

Forming Loops

As the baselines are drawn on the project map for a static GPS survey, or any GPS work where accuracy is the primary consideration, the designer should remember that part of their effectiveness depends on the formation of complete geometric figures. When the project is completed, these independent vectors should be capable of formation into closed loops that incorporate baselines from two to four different sessions. In the illustrated baseline plan, no loop contains more than 10 vectors, no loop is more than 100 km long, and every observed baseline will have a place in a closed loop.

Finding the Number of Sessions

The illustrated survey design calls for 10 sessions, but the calculation does not include human error, equipment breakdown, and other unforeseeable difficulties. It would be impractical to presume a completely trouble-free project. The FGCC proposes the following formula for arriving at a more realistic estimate:

$$ s = \frac{(m \bullet n)}{r} + \frac{(m \bullet n)(p - 1)}{r} + k \bullet m $$

where: s = the number of observing sessions
r = the number of receivers
m = the total number of stations involved.

However, n, p, and k require a bit more explanation. The variable n is a representation of the level of redundancy that has been built into the network, based on the number of occupations on each station. The illustrated survey design includes more than two occupations on all but 4 of the 14 stations in the network. In fact, 10 of the 14 positions will be visited three or four times in the course of the survey. There are a total of 40 occupations by the 4 receivers in the 10 planned sessions. By dividing 40 occupations by 14 stations, it can be found that each station will be visited an average of 2.857 times. Therefore, in the FGCC formula the planned redundancy represented by factor n is equal to 2.857 in this project.

The experience of a firm is symbolized by the variable p in the formula. The division of the final number of actual sessions required to complete past projects by the initial estimation yields a ratio that can be used to improve future predictions. That ratio is the production factor, p. A typical production factor is 1.1.

A safety factor of 0.1, known as k, is recommended for GPS projects within 100 km of a company's homebase. Beyond that radius, an increase to 0.2 is advised.

The substitution of the appropriate quantities for the illustrated project increases the prediction of the number of observation sessions required for its completion:

$$s = \frac{(mn)}{r} + \frac{(mn)(p - 1)}{r} + km$$

$$s = \frac{(14)(2.857)}{4} + \frac{(14)(2.857)(1.1 - 1)}{4} + (0.2)(14)$$

$$s = \frac{40}{4} + \frac{4}{4} + 2.8$$

$$s = 10 + 1 + 2.8$$

$$s = 14 \text{ sessions (rounded to the nearest int eger)}$$

In other words, the 2-day, 10-session schedule is a minimum period for the baseline plan drawn on the project map. A more realistic estimate of the observation schedule includes 14 sessions. It is also important to keep in mind that the observation schedule does not include time for onsite reconnaissance.

Ties to the Vertical Control

The ties from the vertical control stations to the overall network are usually not handled by the same methods used with the horizontal control. The first session of the illustrated project was devoted to occupation of all the horizontal control stations. There is no similar method with the vertical control stations. First, the geoidal undulation would be indistinguishable from baseline measurement error. Second, the primary objective in vertical control is for each station to be adequately tied to its closest neighbor in the network.

If a benchmark can serve as a project point, it is nearly always advisable to use it, as was done with stations 11 and 14 in the illustrated project. A conventional level circuit can often be used to transfer a reliable orthometric elevation from vertical control station to a nearby project point.

Combining GPS Surveying Methods

A mixture of GPS surveying methods is frequently the most efficient approach to a particular project. Static surveying, such as that used in the illustrated project, or pseudokinematic GPS are both well suited to establishing the overall control for a project to set the stage for other methods. For example, they can be used to set control on either side of obstructions to prepare for receiver initialization in later kinematic observations.

Next Chapter

Reconnaissance is a vital ingredient for the success of such surveys. In fact, systematic onsite reconnaissance is one of the most important aspects of any kind of GPS surveying. More about that and other features of actually performing GPS observations will be presented in Chapter 7.

REFERENCES

Federal Geodetic Control Committee. Geometric Geodetic Accuracy and Specifications for Using GPS Relative Positioning Techniques, Version 5, August 1, 1989.

Trimble Navigation Limited. WAVE Baseline Processor and SV Azimuth & Elevation Table. GPSurvey Software Suite. Version 1.10D.

U.S. Department of Commerce, NOAA, National Ocean Survey, National Geodetic Survey. Control Data Sheets.

Chapter Seven

Observing

PREPARING TO OBSERVE

The prospects for the success of a GPS project are directly proportional to the quality and training of the people doing it. The handling of the equipment, the onsite reconnaissance, the creation of field logs, and the inevitable last-minute adjustments to the survey design all depend for their success on the training of the personnel involved. There are those who say the operation of GPS receivers no longer requires highly qualified survey personnel. That might be true if effective GPS surveying needed only the pushing of the appropriate buttons at the appropriate time. In fact, when all goes as planned, it may appear to the uninitiated that GPS has made experienced field surveyors obsolete. But when the unavoidable breakdowns in planning or equipment occur, the capable people, who seemed so superfluous moments before, suddenly become indispensable.

Training

One of the great drawbacks of the education demanded by high technology work of all kinds is the resulting nonbillable time. The often quoted principle that 85 percent of every employee's time ought to be billable is certainly violated during any period of extensive training. GPS presents ever-increasing efficiency and productivity to a surveying operation. But the rate of that growth and change cannot be used to advantage without an equally constant growth in the knowledge of the personnel charged with actually doing the work.

Equipment

Conventional Equipment

Most GPS projects require conventional surveying equipment for spirit-leveling circuits, offsetting horizontal control stations and monumenting project points, among other things. It is perhaps a bit ironic that this most advanced surveying method also frequently has need of the most basic equipment. The use of brush hooks, machetes, axes, etc., can sometimes salvage an otherwise unusable position by removing overhead obstacles. Another strategy for overcoming such hindrances has been developed using various types of survey masts to elevate a separate GPS antenna above the obstructing canopy.

Flagging, paint, and the various techniques of marking that surveyors have developed over the years are still a necessity in GPS work. The pressure of working in unfamiliar terrain is often combined with urgency. Even though there is usually not a moment to spare in moving from station to station, a GPS surveyor frequently does not have the benefit of having visited the particular points before. In such situations, the clear marking of both the route and the station during reconnaissance is vital. Marking the route between stations in kinematic GPS carries the added importance of preventing the loss of the continuous satellite lock essential to the survey's success.

Despite the best route marking, a surveyor may not be able to reach the planned station, or, having arrived, finds some new obstacle or unanticipated problem that can only be solved by marking and occupying an impromptu offset position for a session. A hammer, nails, shiners, paint, etc., are essential in such situations.

In short, the full range of conventional surveying equipment and expertise have a place in GPS. For some, their role may be more abbreviated than it was formerly, but one element that can never be outdated is good judgment.

Safety Equipment

The high-visibility vests, cones, lights, flagmen, and signs needed for traffic control cannot be neglected in GPS work. Unlike conventional surveying operations, GPS observations are not deterred by harsh weather. Occupying a control station in a highway is dangerous enough under the best of conditions, but in the midst of a rainstorm, fog, or blizzard, it can be absolute folly without the proper precautions. And any time and trouble taken to avoid infraction of the local regulations regarding traffic management will be compensated by an uninterrupted observation schedule.

Weather conditions also affect travel between the stations of the survey, both in vehicles and on foot. Equipment and plans to deal with emergencies should be part of any GPS project. First aid kits, fire extinguishers, and the usual safety equipment are necessary. Training in safety procedures can be an extraordinary benefit, but perhaps the most important capability in an emergency is communication.

Communications

Whether the equipment is handheld or vehicle mounted, two-way radios are used in most GPS operations. However, the line of sight that is no longer necessary for the surveying measurements in GPS is sorely missed in the effort to maintain clear radio contact between the receiver operators. A radio link between surveyors can increase the efficiency and safety of a GPS project, but it is particularly valuable when last-minute changes in the observation schedule are necessary. When an observer is unable to reach a station or a receiver suddenly becomes inoperable, unless adjustments to the schedule can be made quickly, each end of all of the lines into the missed station will require reobservation.

Unless a receiver is collecting data continuously at a foothold or master station, communication is particularly important in pseudokinematic surveys. The success of both pseudokinematic and all types of static GPS hinges on all receivers collecting their data simultaneously. However, it is more and more difficult to ensure reliable communication between receiver operators in geodetic surveys, especially as their lines grow longer.

One alternative to contact between surveyors is reliance on the pre-programming feature available on most GPS receivers today. This attribute usually allows the start-stop time, sampling rate, bandwidth, satellites to track, mask angle, data file name, and start position to be preset so that the operator need only set up the receiver at the appropriate station before the session begins. The receiver is expected to handle the rest automatically. In theory, this approach eliminates the chance for an operator error ruining an observation session by missing the time to power-up, or improperly entering the other information. Theory falls short of practice here, and even if the procedure could eliminate those mistakes, entire categories of other errors remain unaddressed. Some advocate actually leaving receivers unattended in static GPS. This idea seems unwise on the face of it.

High-wattage, private-line FM radios are quite useful when line of sight is available between them or when a repeater is available. The use of portable telephones may eliminate the communication problem in some areas, but probably not in remote locations. Despite the limitations of the systems available at the moment, achievement of the best possible communication between surveyors on a GPS project pays dividends in the long run.

GPS Equipment

Most GPS receivers capable of geodetic accuracy are designed to be mounted on a tripod, usually with a tribrach and adaptor. However, there is a trend toward bipod- or range-pole-mounted antennas. Some of these arrangements are designed for easy vehicle mounting to facilitate the quick setups needed in kinematic or pseudokinematic applications. Another advantage of these devices is that they ensure a constant height of the antenna above the station. The mismeasured height of the antenna above the mark is one of the most pervasive blunders in GPS.

The tape or rod used to measure the height of the antenna is sometimes built into the receiver, and sometimes a separate device. It is important that the H.I. be measured accurately and consistently in both feet and meters, without merely converting from one to the other mathematically. It is also important that the value be recorded in the field notes and, where possible, also entered into the receiver itself.

Where tribrachs are used to mount the antenna, the tribrach's optical centering should be checked and calibrated. It is critical that the effort to perform GPS surveys to an accuracy of centimeters not be frustrated by inaccurate centering or H.I. measurement. Since many systems measure the height of the antenna to the edge of the ground plane or to the exterior of the receiver itself, the calibration of the tribrach affects both the centering and the H.I. measurement. The resetting of a receiver that occupies the same station in consecutive sessions is an important source of redundancy for many kinds of GPS networks. However, integrity can only be added if the tribrach has been accurately calibrated.

The checking of the receivers themselves is also critical to the control of errors in a GPS survey, especially when different receivers or different models of antennas are to be used on the same work. The zero baseline test is a method that may be used to fulfill equipment calibration specifications where a three-dimensional test network of sufficient accuracy is not available. This test can also be used to separate receiver difficulties from antenna errors.

Two or more receivers are connected to one antenna with a signal splitter. An observation is done with the divided signal from the single antenna reaching both receivers simultaneously. After processing, if the measured length of the baseline is confirmed to be zero, the health of both of the receivers' electronics is corroborated. The success of this test depends on the signal from one antenna reaching both receivers, but the current from only one receiver can be allowed to power the antenna.

Auxiliary Equipment

Tools to repair the ends of connecting cables, a simple pencil eraser to clean the contacts of circuit boards, or any of a number of small implements have saved more than one GPS observation session from failure. Experience has shown that GPS surveying requires at least as much resourcefulness, if not more, than conventional surveying.

The health of the batteries is a constant concern in GPS. There is simply nothing to be done when a receiver's battery is drained but to resume power as soon as possible. A backup power source is essential. Cables to connect a vehicle battery, an extra fully-charged battery unit, or both should be immediately available to every receiver operator.

Papers

The papers every GPS observer carries throughout a project ought to include emergency phone numbers; the names, addresses, and phone numbers of relevant property owners; and the combinations to necessary locks. Each member of the team should also have a copy of the project map, any other maps that are needed to clarify position or access, and, perhaps most important of all, the updated observation schedule.

The observation schedule will be revised daily based upon actual production (Table 7.1). It should specify the start-stop times and station for all the personnel during each session of the upcoming day. In this way, the schedule will not only serve to inform every receiver operator of his or her own expected occupations, but those of every other member of the project as well. This knowledge is most useful when a sudden revision requires observers to meet or replace one another.

RECONNAISSANCE

Station Data Sheet

The principles of good field notes have a long tradition in land surveying, and they will continue to have validity for some time to come. In GPS,

Table 7.1. Observation Schedule—Day 49

	Session 1 Start 7:10 Stop 8:10	8:10 to 8:40	Session 2 Start 8:40 Stop 9:50	9:50 to 10:15	Session 3 Start 10:15 Stop 11:15	11:15 to 11:30	Session 4 Start 11:30 Stop 12:30	12:30 to 14:00	Session 5 Start 14:00 Stop 15:00
SVs PRNs	9,12,13,16,20,24		3,12,13,16,20,24		3,12,13,16,17,20,24		3,16,17,20,22,23,26		1,3,17,21,23,26,28
Receiver A Dan H.	Station 1 NGS Horiz. Control	Re-Set	Station 1 NGS Horiz. Control	Move	Station 5 NGS Benchmark	Re-Set	Station 5 NGS Benchmark	Re-Set	Station 5 NGS Benchmark
Receiver B Scott G.	Station 3 NGS V&H Control	Re-Set	Station 3 NGS V&H Control	Move	Station 6 Project Point	Re-Set	Station 6 Project Point	Move	Station 1 NGS Horiz. Control
Receiver C Dewey A.	Station 8 NGS Horiz. Control	Move	Station 2 Project Point	Re-Set	Station 2 Project Point	Move	Station 7 Project Point	Move	Station 10 NGS Benchmark
Receiver D Cindy B.	Station 13 NGS Horiz. Control	Move	Station 4 Project Point	Re-Set	Station 4 Project Point	Move	Station 9 Project Point	Move	Station 13 NGS Horiz. Control

the ensuing paper trail will not only fill subsequent archives; it has immediate utility. For example, the station data sheet is often an important bridge between onsite reconnaissance and the actual occupation of a monument.

Though every organization develops its own unique system of handling its field records, most have some form of the station data sheet. The document illustrated in Figure 7.1 is merely one possible arrangement of the information needed to recover the station.

The station data sheet can be prepared at any period of the project, but perhaps the most usual times are during the reconnaissance of existing control or immediately after the monumentation of a new project point. Neatness and clarity, always paramount virtues of good field notes, are of particular interest when the station data sheet is to be later included in the final report to the client. The overriding principle in drafting a station data sheet is to guide succeeding visitors to the station without ambiguity. A GPS surveyor on the way to observe the position for the first time may be the initial user of a station data sheet. A poorly written document could void an entire session if the observer is unable to locate the monument. A client, later struggling to find a particular monument with an inadequate data sheet, may ultimately question the value of more than the field notes.

Station Name

The station name fills the first blank on the illustrated data sheet. Two names for a single monument is far from unusual. In this case, the vertical control station, officially named S 198, is also serving as a project point, number 14. But two names purporting to represent the same position can present a difficulty. For example, when a horizontal control station is remonumented, a number 2 is sometimes added to the original name of the station and it can be confusing. For example, it can be easy to mistake station "Thornton 2" with an original station named "Thornton" that no longer exists. Both stations may still have a place in the published record, but with slightly different coordinates. Another unfortunate misunderstanding can occur when inexperienced field personnel mistake a reference mark, R.M., for the actual station itself. The taking of rubbings and/or close-up photographs is widely recommended to avoid such blunders regarding stations' names or authority.

Rubbings

The illustrated station data sheet provides an area to accommodate a rubbing. With the paper held on top of the monument's disk, a pencil is run

STATION DATA SHEET

Station Name: _S 198 (PROJECT POINT 14)_

USGS Quad: _BEND_ _____ Year Monumented: _1948_

Described By: _S. GRAHAM_ _____ Year Recovered: _1994_

State/County: _MONTANA / FLATHEAD COUNTY_

Stamped   Sketch

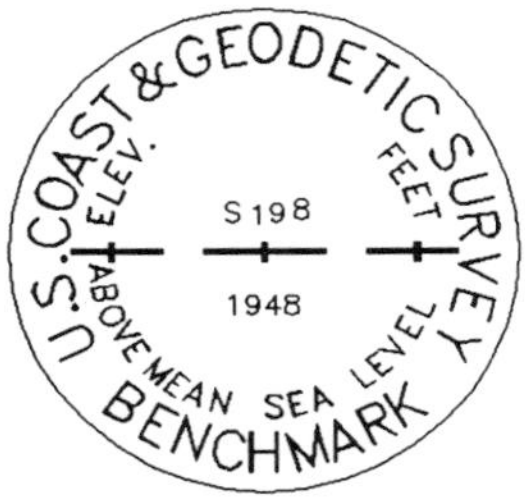

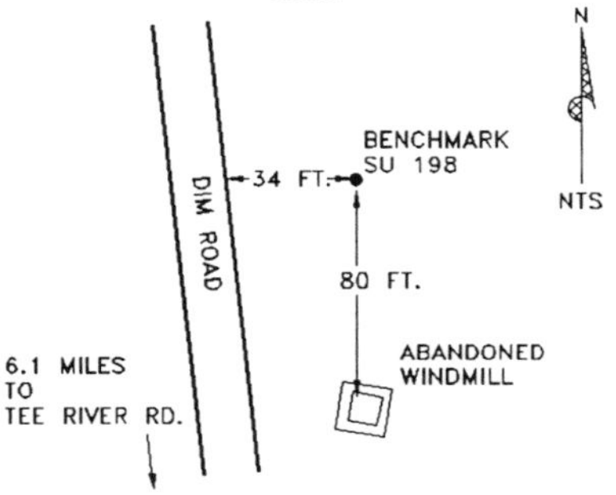

To Reach:

The station is located about 9 miles southeast of the Dew Drop Inn

and about 2 miles south of the Bend Guard Station. To reach from the Dew

Drop Inn, go southeast from the junction of U.S. Highway 2 and the Tee River

Rd. (State Hwy. 20) 14 miles on the Tee River Rd. to a Y-junction with a dim

road. Turn left (northwest) onto dim road and travel 6.1 miles to an abandoned

windmill.   Station is 80 feet north of the windmill, 34 feet east of the road.

Monument Description:

Station mark is a standard metal disk set in a concrete post protruding

3 inches above the ground.   The disk is stamped "S 198 1948."

_____   _2/17/94_
Signature   Date

Figure 7.1. Station Data Sheet.

over it in a zigzag pattern, producing a positive image of the stamping. This method is a bit more awkward than simply copying the information from the disk onto the data sheet, but it does have the advantage of ensuring the station was actually visited and that the stamping was faithfully recorded. Such rubbings or close-up photographs are required by the provisional FGCC

Geometric Geodetic Accuracy Standards and Specifications for Using GPS Relative Positioning Techniques for all orders of GPS surveys.

Photographs

The use of photographs is growing as a help for the perpetuation of monuments. It can be convenient to photograph the area around the mark as well as the monument itself. These exposures can be correlated with a sketch of the area. Such a sketch can show the spot where the photographer stood and the directions toward which the pictures were taken. The photographs can then provide valuable information in locating monuments, even if they are later obscured. Still, the traditional ties to prominent features in the area around the mark are the primary agent of their recovery.

Quad Sheet Name

Providing the name of the appropriate state, county, and USGS quad sheet helps to correlate the station data sheet with the project map. The year the mark was monumented, the monument description, the station name, and the "to-reach" description all help to associate the information with the correct official control data sheet and, most importantly, the correct station coordinates.

To-Reach Descriptions

The description of the route to the station is one of the most critical documents written during the reconnaissance. Even though it is difficult to prepare the information in unfamiliar territory and although every situation is somewhat different, there are some guidelines to be followed. It is best to begin with the general location of the station with respect to easily found local features.

The description in Figure 7.1 relies on a road junction, a guard station, and a local business. After defining the general location of the monument, the description should recount directions for reaching the station. Starting from a prominent location, the directions should adequately describe the roads and junctions. Where the route is difficult or confusing, the reconnaissance team should not only describe the junctions and turns needed to reach a station, it is wise to also mark them with lath and flagging, when possible. It is also a good idea to note gates. Even if they are open during reconnaissance, they may be locked later. When turns are called for, it is best to describe not only the direction of the turn, but the new course too.

For example, in the description in Figure 7.1 the turn onto the dim road from the Tee River Road is described to the "left (northwest)." Roads and highways should carry both local names and designations found on standard highway maps. For example, in Figure 7.1 Tee River Road is also described as State Highway 20.

The "to-reach" description should certainly state the mileages as well as the travel times where they are appropriate, particularly where packing-in is required. Land ownership, especially if the owner's consent is required for access, should be mentioned. The reconnaissance party should obtain the permission to enter private property and should inform the GPS observer of any conditions of that entry. Alternate routes should be described where they may become necessary. It is also best to make special mention of any route that is likely to be difficult in inclement weather.

Where helicopter access is anticipated, information about the duration of flights from point to point, the distance of landing sites from the station, and flight time to fuel supplies should be included on the station data sheet.

Flagging and Describing the Monument

Flagging the station during reconnaissance may help the observer find the mark more quickly. On the station data sheet, the detailed description of the location of the station with respect to roads, fence lines, buildings, trees, and any other conspicuous features should include measured distances and directions. A clear description of the monument itself is important. It is wise to also show and describe any nearby marks, such as R.M.s, that may be mistaken for the station or aid in its recovery. The name of the preparer, a signature, and the date round out the initial documentation of a GPS station.

Visibility Diagrams

Obstructions above the mask angle of a GPS receiver must be taken into account in finalizing the observation schedule. A station that is blocked to some degree is not necessarily unusable, but its inclusion in any particular session is probably contingent on the position of the specific satellites involved.

An Example

The diagram in Figure 7.2 is widely used to record such obstructions during reconnaissance. It is known as a *station visibility diagram*, a *po-*

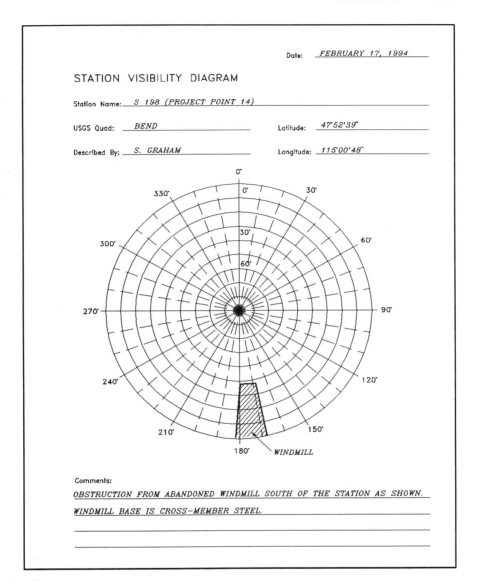

Figure 7.2. Station Visibility Diagram.

lar plot or a *skyplot*. The concentric circles are meant to indicate 10°
increments along the upper half of the celestial sphere, from the observer's
horizon at 0° on the perimeter, to the observer's zenith at 90° in the center.
The hemisphere is cut by the observer's meridian, shown as a line from

0°in the north to 180° on the south. The prime vertical is signified as the line from 90° in the east to 270° in the west. The other numbers and solid lines radiating from the center, every 30° around the perimeter of the figure, are azimuths from north and are augmented by dashed lines every 10°.

Drawing Obstructions

Using a compass and a clinometer, a member of the reconnaissance team can fully describe possible obstructions of the satellite's signals on a visibility diagram. By standing at the station mark and measuring the azimuth and vertical angle of points outlining the obstruction, the observer can plot the object on the visibility diagram. For example, a windmill base is shown in Figure 7.2 as a cross-hatched figure. It has been drawn from the observer's horizon up to 37° in vertical angle from 168°, to about 182° in azimuth at its widest point. This description by approximate angular values is entirely adequate for determining when particular satellites may be blocked at this station.

For example, suppose a 1-hour session from 9:10 to 10:10, illustrated in Table 7.2, was under consideration for the observation on station S 198. The station visibility chart might motivate a careful look at SV PRN 16. Twenty minutes into the anticipated session, at 9:30, SV 16 has just risen above the 15° mask angle. Under normal circumstances, it would be available at station S 198, but it appears from the polar plot that the windmill will block its signals from reaching the receiver. In fact, the signals from SV 16 will apparently not reach station S 198 until sometime after the end of the session at 10:10.

Working Around Obstructions

Under the circumstances, some consideration might be given to observing station S 198 during a session when none of the satellites would be blocked. However, the 9:10 to 10:10 session may be adequate after all. Even if SV 16 is completely blocked, the remaining five satellites will be unobstructed, and the constellation still will have a relatively low PDOP. Still, the analysis must be carried to other stations that will be occupied during the same session. The success of the measurement of any baseline depends on common observations at both ends of the line. Therefore, if the signals from SV 16 are garbled or blocked from station S 198, any information collected during the same session from that satellite at the other end of a line that includes S 198 will be useless in processing the vector between those two stations.

Table 7.2. Satellites Azimuth and Elevation Table (Plot 1=1.1)

Satellites
Azimuth and Elevation Table

Time	SV 3 El	Az	SV 12 El	Az	SV 13 El	Az	SV 16 El	Az	SV 20 El	Az	SV 24 El	Az	PDOP
constellation of 5 SVs													
8:50	54	235	74	274	44	28			16	308	68	169	4.8
9:00	51	229	74	255	40	32			20	310	72	163	5.7
9:10	47	224	72	238	37	35			23	311	77	153	4.9
9:20	43	219	68	226	33	38			27	313	80	134	4.0
constellation of 6 SVs													
9:30	39	215	64	218	29	41	16	179	31	314	81	102	2.1
9:40	35	212	59	213	26	45	19	176	36	314	80	73	2.3
9:50	31	209	54	209	23	48	23	173	40	315	76	57	2.4
10:00	27	207	49	206	19	52	27	170	44	314	72	49	2.5
10:10	23	204	44	204	16	55	30	167	48	314	67	45	2.5

But the material of the base of the abandoned windmill has been described on the visibility diagram as cross-membered steel, so it is possible that the signal from SV 16 will not be entirely obstructed during the whole session. There may actually be more concern of multipath interference from the structure than that of signal availability. One strategy for handling the situation might be to program the receiver at S 198 to ignore the signal from SV 16 completely.

The visibility diagram (Figure 7.2) and the azimuth-elevation table (Table 7.2) complement each other. They provide the field supervisor with the data needed to make informed judgments about the observation schedule. Even if the decision is taken to include station S 198 in the 9:10 to 10:10 session as originally planned, the supervisor will be forewarned that the blockage of SV 16 may introduce a bit of weakness at that particular station.

Approximate Station Coordinates

The latitude and longitude given on the station visibility diagram should be understood to be approximate. It is sometimes a scaled coordinate, or it may be taken from another source. In either case, its primary role is as input for the receiver at the beginning of its observation. The coordinate need only be close enough to the actual position of the receiver to minimize the time the receiver must take to lock onto the constellation of satellites it expects to find.

Multipath

The multipath condition is by no means unique to GPS. When a transmitted television signal reaches the receiving antenna by two or more paths, the resulting variations in amplitude and phase cause the picture to have ghosts. This kind of scattering of the signals can be caused by reflection from land, water, or man-made structures. In GPS, the problem can be particularly troublesome when signals are received from satellites at low elevation angles; hence, the general use of a 15° to 20° mask angle.

It is also wise, where it is possible, to avoid using stations that are near structures likely to be reflective or to scatter the signal. For example, chain-link fences that are found hard against a mark can cause multipath by forcing the satellite's signal to pass through the mesh to reach the antenna. The elevation of the antenna over the top of the fence with a survey mast is often the best way to work around this kind of obstruction. Metal structures with large flat surfaces are notorious for causing multipath problems.

Offsets well away from such a building are probably the best solution. A long train moving near a project point could be a potential problem, but vehicles passing by on a highway or street usually are not, especially if they go by at high speed. It is important, of course, to avoid parked vehicles. It is best to remind new GPS observers that the survey vehicle should be parked far enough from the point to avert any multipath.

Look for Multipath

Both the GPS field supervisor and the reconnaissance team should be alert to any indications on the station visibility diagram that multipath may be a concern. Before the observations are done, there is nearly always a simple solution. Discovering multipath in the signals after the observations are done is not only frustrating, but often expensive.

Reconnaissance for Kinematic GPS

A careful reconnaissance of the routes between stations is required for successful kinematic GPS. Clear sky for at least five satellites 20° or more above the horizon is a necessity to maintain an adequate lock throughout the survey. Unavoidable obstructions like bridges and tunnels can be overcome by the placement of the control station on both sides of the barrier. If these control stations are coordinated by some type of static observation, they can later be used to re-initialize the kinematic receivers.

Monumentation

The monumentation set for GPS projects varies widely and can range from brass tablets to aerial premarks, capped rebar, or even pin flags. The objective of most station markers is to adequately serve the client's subsequent use. However, the time, trouble, and cost in most high-accuracy GPS work warrants the most permanent, stable monumentation.

Many experts predict that GPS will eventually make monumentation unnecessary. The idea foresees GPS receivers in constant operation at well-known master stations will allow surveyors with receivers to determine highly accurate relative positions with such speed and ease that monumentation will be unnecessary. The idea may prove prophetic, but for now, monumentation is an important part of most GPS projects. The suitability of a particular type of monument is an area still most often left to the professional judgment of the surveyors involved.

The FGCC recommends the use of traditional metal disks set in rock outcroppings, bridge abutments, or other large structural elements where possible. A three-dimensional rod mark is approved as an alternative by the federal committee. It is described in detail in Appendix H of *Geometric Geodetic Accuracy Standards and Specifications for Using GPS Relative Positioning Techniques.*

FINAL PLANNING AND OBSERVATION

Logistics

Scheduling

Once all the station data sheets, visibility diagrams, and other field notes have been collected, the schedule can be finalized for the first observations. There will almost certainly be changes from the original plan. Some of the anticipated control stations may be unavailable or obstructed, some project points may be blocked, too difficult to reach, or simply not serve the purpose as well as a control station at an alternate location. When the final control has been chosen, the project points have been monumented, and the reconnaissance has been completed, the information can be brought together with some degree of certainty that it represents the actual conditions in the field.

Now that the access and travel time, the length of vectors, and the actual obstructions are more certainly known, the length and order of the sessions can be solidified. Despite all the care and planning that goes into preparing for a project, unexpected changes in the satellite's orbits or health can upset the best schedule at the last minute. It is always helpful to have a backup plan.

The receiver operators usually have been involved in the reconnaissance and are familiar with the area and many of the stations. Even though an observer may not have visited the particular stations scheduled for him, the copies of the project map, appropriate station data sheets, and visibility diagrams will usually prove adequate to their location.

Observation

When everything goes as planned, a GPS observation is uneventful. However, even before the arrival of the receiver operator at the control or project point the session can get offtrack. The simultaneity of the data collected at each end of a baseline is critical to the success of any measurement in GPS. When a receiver occupies a master station throughout a project, there need be little concern on this subject. But most static applications depend on the sessions of many mobile receivers beginning and ending together.

Arrival

The number of possible delays that may befall an observer on the way to a station are too numerous to mention. With proper planning and reconnaissance, the observer will likely find that there is enough time for the trip from station to station and that sufficient information is on hand to guide him to the position, but this too cannot be guaranteed. When the observer is late to the station, the best course is usually to set up the receiver quickly and collect as much data as possible. The baselines into the late station may or may not be saved, but they will certainly be lost if the receiver operator collects no information at all. It is at times like these that good communication between the members of the GPS team are most useful. For example, some of the other observers in the session may be able to stay on their station a bit longer with the late arrival, and make up some of the lost data. Along the same line, it is usually a good policy for those operators who are to remain on a station for two consecutive sessions to collect data as long as possible, while still leaving themselves enough time to reset between the two observation periods.

Setup

Centering an instrument over the station mark is always important. However, the centimeter-level accuracy of static GPS gives the centering of the antenna special significance. It is ironic that such a sophisticated system of surveying can be defeated from such a commonplace procedure. A tribrach with an optical plummet or any other device used for centering should be checked and, if necessary, adjusted before the project begins. With good centering and leveling procedures, an antenna should be within a few millimeters of the station mark. The FGCC's provisional specifications require that the antenna's centering be checked with a plumb bob at each station for surveys of the AA, A, and B orders.

Unfortunately, the centering of the antenna over the station does not ensure that its phase center is properly oriented. The contours of equal phase around the antenna's electronic center are not themselves perfectly spherical. Part of their eccentricity can be attributed to unavoidable inaccuracies in the manufacturing process. To compensate for some of this offset, it is a good practice to rotate all antennas in a session to the same direction. Many manufacturers provide reference marks on their antennas so that each one may be oriented to the same azimuth. That way, they are expected to maintain the same relative position between their physical and electronic centers when observations are made.

The antenna's configuration also affects another measurement critical to successful GPS surveying: the height of the instrument. The frequency of mistakes in this important measurement is remarkable. Several methods have been devised to focus special attention on the height of the antenna. Not only should it be measured in both feet and meters, it should also be measured immediately after the instrument is set up and just before tearing it down, to detect any settling of the tripod during the observation.

Height of Instrument

The measurement of the height of the antenna in a GPS survey is often not made on a plumb line. A tape is frequently stretched from the top of the station monument to some reference mark on the antenna or the receiver itself. Some GPS teams measure and record the height of the antenna to more than one reference mark on the ground plane. These measurements are usually mathematically corrected to plumb.

The care ascribed to the measurement of antenna heights is due to the same concern applied to centering. GPS has an extraordinary capability to achieve accurate heights, but those heights can be easily contaminated by incorrect H.I.s.

Observation Logs

Most GPS operations require its receiver operators to keep a careful log of each observation. Usually written on a standard form, these field notes provide a written record of the measurements, times, equipment, and other data that explain what actually occurred during the observation itself. It is difficult to overestimate the importance of this information. It is usually incorporated into the final report of the survey, the archives, and any subsequent effort to blue-book the project. However, the most immediate use of the observation log is in the evaluation of the day's work by the onsite field supervisor.

An observation log may be organized in a number of ways. The log illustrated in Figure 7.3 is one method that includes some of the information that might be used to document one session at one station. Of course, the name of the observer and the station must be included, and while the

OBSERVATION LOG

JOB NUMBER | ULY2396

OBSERVER	STATION	JULIAN DATE	DATE
S. GRAHAM	S 198 (POINT 14)	50	2/17/94

LATITUDE	LONGITUDE	HEIGHT
47°52'39"	115°00'48"	3241.09 FT.

PLANNED OBSERVATION SESSION	SESSION NAME	ACTUAL OBSERVATION SESSION
START TIME: 9:10 STOP TIME: 10:10	0014 050 2	START TIME: 9:10 STOP TIME: 10:10

ANTENNA TYPE	ANTENNA HEIGHT ABOVE STATION MONUMENT	
ON-BOARD	BEFORE OBSERVATION	AFTER OBSERVATION
	METERS: 1.585	METERS: 1.585
MASK ANGLE: 15°	FEET: 5.20	FEET: 5.20

METEOROLOGICAL DATA				
TIME	RELATIVE HUMIDITY	BAROMETER	THERMOMETER (D)	THERMOMETER (W)
9:30	30%	29.94	37 F	35 F

VISIBILITY DIAGRAM COMPLETED? (Y) N   TOP OF MONUMENT ABOVE THE SURFACE: 3 IN.

STATION DATA SHEET COMPLETED? (Y) N   TOP OF MONUMENT BELOW THE SURFACE:

SV PRN TRACKED		COMMENTS:
3	16	DATA FROM SV 16 APPEARS HEALTHY
12	20	DESPITE WINDMILL OBSTRUCTION.
13	24	

Figure 7.3. Observation Log.

date need not be expressed in both the Julian and Gregorian calendars, that information may help in quick cataloging of the data. The approximate latitude, longitude, and height of the station are usually required by the receiver as a reference position for its search for satellites. The date of the planned session will not necessarily coincide with the actual session observed. The observer's arrival at the point may have been late, or the receiver may have been allowed to collect data beyond the scheduled end of the session.

There are various methods used to name observation sessions in terminology that is sensible to computers. A widely used system is noted here. The first four digits are the project point's number. In this case, it is point 14 and is designated 0014. The next three digits are the Julian day of the session; in this case, it is day 50, or 050. Finally, the session illustrated is the second of the day, or 2. Therefore, the full session name is 0014 050 2.

Whether onboard or separate, the type of the antenna used and the height of the antenna are critical pieces of information. The relation of the height of the station to the height of the antenna is vital to the station's later utility. The distance that the top of the station's monument is found above or below the surface of the surrounding soil is sometimes neglected. This information can not only be useful in later recovery of the monument, but can also be important in the proper evaluation of photo-control panel points.

Weather

The meteorological data are useful in modeling the atmospheric delay. This information is required at the beginning, middle, and end of each session of projects that are designed to satisfy the FGCC's provisional specifications for the AA and A orders of accuracy. Under those circumstances, measurement of the atmospheric pressure in millibars, the relative humidity, and the temperature in degrees Centigrade are expected to be included in the observation log. However, the general use is less stringent. The conditions of the day are observed, and unusual changes in the weather are noted.

A record of the satellites that are actually available during the observation, and any comments about unique circumstances of the session round out the observation log.

Daily Progress Evaluation

The planned observation schedules of a large GPS project usually change daily. The arrangements of upcoming sessions are often altered, based on the success or failure of the previous day's plan. Such a regrouping follows evaluation of the day's data.

This evaluation involves examination of the observation logs as well as the data each receiver has collected. Unhealthy data, caused by cycle slips or any other source, are not always apparent to the receiver operator at the time of the observation. Therefore, a daily quality control check is a necessary preliminary step before finalizing the next day's observation schedule.

Some field supervisors prefer to actually compute the independent baseline vectors of each day's work to ensure that the measurements are adequate. Neglecting the daily check could leave unsuccessful sessions undiscovered until the survey was thought to be completed. The consequences of such a situation could be expensive.

REFERENCES

Federal Geodetic Control Committee. Geometric Geodetic Accuracy Standards and Specifications for Using GPS Relative Positioning Techniques, Version 5, Aug. 1, 1989.

Trimble Navigation Limited. Model 4000ST GPS Surveyor, Operation Manual, July 1989 3.2X, page D-1.

Chapter Eight

Postmission Processing

PROCESSING

In many ways, processing is the heart of a GPS operation. Some processing should be performed on a daily basis during a GPS project. Blunders from operators, noisy data, and unhealthy satellites can corrupt entire sessions, and left undetected, such dissolution can jeopardize an entire survey. But with some daily processing, these weaknesses in the data can be discovered when they can still be eliminated with a timely amendment of the observation schedule.

But even after blunders and noisy data have been removed from the observation sets, GPS measurements are still composed of fundamentally biased ranges. Therefore, GPS data-processing procedures are really a series of interconnected computerized operations designed to remove these more difficult biases and extract the true ranges.

The biases originate from a number of sources: imperfect clocks, atmospheric delays, cycle ambiguities in carrier phase observations, and orbital errors. If a bias has a stable, well-understood structure, it can be estimated together with the station coordinates. In other cases, dual-frequency observations can be used to measure the bias directly, as in the ionospheric delay,or a model may be used to predict an effect, as in tropospheric delay. But one of the most effective strategies in eradicating biases is called *differencing*.

Correlation of Biases

When two or more receivers observe the same satellite constellation simultaneously, a set of correlated vectors is created between the co-observing stations. Most GPS practitioners use more than two receivers. Therefore, most GPS networks consist of many sets of correlated vectors for every separate session. The longest baselines between stations on the earth are usually relatively short when compared with the 20,000-km distances from the receivers to the GPS satellites. Therefore, even when several receivers are set up on widely spaced stations, as long as they collect their data simultaneously from the same constellation of satellites, they will record very similar errors. In other words, their vectors will be correlated. It is the simultaneity of observation and the resulting correlation of the carrier phase observables that make the extraordinary GPS accuracies possible. Biases that are correlated linearly can be virtually eliminated by differencing the data sets of a session.

It is this double and triple differencing of carrier phase observations derived from static receivers that will be presented in more detail in this chapter; then there will be some discussion of the methods of coping with cycle slips.

Once the station vectors have been derived from carrier phase solutions, their reliability is usually checked by combining several of them in a minimally constrained least-squares solution. This procedure is sometimes followed by an adjustment of the orbits of the GPS satellitesthemselves, when the highest possible positional accuracy is required.

Quantity of Data

Organization Is Essential

One of the difficulties of GPS processing is the huge amount of data that must be managed. For example, when even one single-frequency receiver with a 1-second sampling rate tracks one GPS satellite for an hour, it collects about 0.15 Mb of data. However, a more realistic scenario involves four receivers observing six satellites for 3600 epochs. There can be 4 X 6 X 3600 or 86,400 carrier phase observations in such a session. In other words, a real-life GPS survey with many sessions and many baselines creates a quantity of data in the gigabyte range. Some sort of structured approach must be implemented to process such a huge amount of information in a reasonable amount of time.

File-Naming Conventions

One aspect of that structure is the naming conventions used to head GPS receivers' observation files. Many manufacturers recommend a file-naming format that can be symbolized by *pppp-ddd-s.yyf*. The first letters, (*pppp*), of the file name indicate the point number of the station occupied. The day of the year, or Julian date, can be accommodated in the next three places (*ddd*), and the final place left of the period is the session number (*s*). The year (*yy*), and the file type (*f*) are sometimes added to the right of the period.

Downloading

The first step in GPS data processing is downloading the collected data from the internal memory of the receiver itself into a PC or laptop computer. When the observations sessions have been completed for the day, each receiver, in turn, is cabled to the computer and its data transferred. Nearly all GPS systems used in surveying are PC-compatible and can accommodate postprocessing in the field. But none can protect the user from a failure to back up this raw observational data onto floppy disks, or some other form of semipermanent storage.

Making Room

Receiver memory capacity is usually somewhat limited, and older data must be cleared to make room for new sessions. Still, it is a good policy to create the necessary space with the minimum deletion and restrict it to only the oldest files in the receiver's memory. In this way the recent data can be retained as long as possible; the data can provide an auxiliary backup system. But when a receiver's memory is finally wiped of a particular session, if redundant raw data are not available, reobservation may be the only remedy.

Most GPS receivers record data internally. Disk storage is the norm, though some rely on cassettes or solid-state memory cards. The Navigation message, meteorological data, the observables, and all other raw data are usually in a manufacturer-specific, binary form. These raw data are usually saved in several distinct files. For example, the PC operator will likely find that the phase measurements downloaded from the receiver will reside in one file and the satellite's ephemeris data in another. Likewise, the measured pseudorange information may be found in itsown dedicated file, the ionospheric information in another, and so on. The particular division of the raw data files is designed to accommodate the suite of processing software and the data management system that the manufacturer has provided its customers, so each will be somewhat unique.

Control

All postprocessing software suites require control. Control is usually entered in the degrees, minutes, and seconds of latitude and longitude and orthometric height, but most will also accept other formats.

The First Position

Baseline processing is usually begun with a point position solution at each end from pseudoranges. These differential code estimations of the approximate position of each receiver antenna can be thought of as establishing a search area, a three-dimensional volume of uncertainty at each receiver containing its correct position. The size of this search area is defined by the accuracy of the code solution, which also affects the computational time required to find the correct position among all the other potential solutions.

Triple Difference

The next step, usually the triple-difference, utilizes the carrier phase observable. Triple differences have several features to recommend them for this stage in the processing. They can achieve rather high accuracy even before cycle slips have been eliminated from the data sets, and they are insensitive to integer ambiguities in general.

Components of a Triple Difference

A triple difference is created by differencing two double differences at each end of the baseline. Each of the double differences involves two satellites and two receivers. A triple difference considers two double differences over two consecutive epochs. In other words, triple differences are formed by sequentially differencing double differences in time. For example, two triple differences can be created using double differences at epochs 1, 2, and 3. One is double difference 2 minus double difference 1. A second can be formed by double difference 3 minus double difference 2.

Since two receivers are recording the data from the same two satellites during two consecutive epochs across a baseline, a triple difference can temporarily eliminate any concern about the integer cycle ambiguity, because the cycle ambiguity is the same over the two observed epochs. However, the triple difference cannot have as much information content as a double difference. Therefore, while receiver coordinates estimated from triple differences are usually more accurate than pseudorange solutions, they are less accurate than those obtained from double differences, especially fixed-ambiguity solutions. Nevertheless, the estimates that come out of triple-difference solutions refine receiver coordinates and provide a starting point for the subsequent double-difference solutions. They are also very useful in spotting and correcting cycle slips.

Double Difference

The next baseline processing steps usually involve two types of double differences, called the *float* and the *fixed* solutions.

The Integer Ambiguity

Double differences have both positive and negative features. On the positive side, they make the highest GPS accuracy possible, and they remove the satellite and receiver clock errors from the observations. On the other hand, the integer cycle ambiguity, sometimes known simply as *the ambiguity*, cannot be ignored in the double difference. In fact, the fixed double-difference solution, usually the most accurate technique of all, requires the resolution of this ambiguity.

The integer cycle ambiguity, usually symbolized by N, represents the number of full phase cycles between the receiver and the satellite at the first instant of the receiver's lock-on. N does not change from the moment the lock is achieved, unless there is a cycle slip. Unfortunately, N is also an unknown quantity at the beginning of any carrier phase observation.

The Float Solution

Once again, estimation plays a significant role in finding the appropriateinteger value that will correctly resolve the ambiguity for component pairs in double differencing. In this first try, there is no effort to translate the biases into integers. It is sometimes said that the integers are allowed to float; hence the initial process is called the *float solution*. Especially when phase measurements for only one frequency, L1 or L2, are available, a sort of calculated guess at the ambiguity is the most direct route to the correct solution. Not just N, but a number of unknowns, such as clock parameters and point coordinates, are estimated in this geometric approach. However, all of these estimated biases are affected by unmodeled errors, and that causes the integer nature of N to be obscured. In other words, the initial estimation of N in a float solution is likely to appear as a real number rather than an integer.

However, where the data are sufficient, these floating real-number estimates are very close to integers—so close that they can next be rounded to their true integer values in a second adjustment of the data. Therefore, a second double-difference solution follows. The estimation of N that is closest to an integer and has the minimum standard error is usually taken to be the most reliable and is rounded to the nearest integer. Now, with one less unknown, the process is repeated and another ambiguity can be fixed, and so on.

The Fixed Solution

This approach is called the *fixed solution* because now the biases can be held to integer values. It is usually quite successful in double differences over short baselines. The resulting fixed solutions most often provide much more accurate results than were available from the initial floating estimates.

Cycle Slip Detection and Repair

However, this process can be corrupted by the presence of cycle slips. A cycle slip is a discontinuity in a receiver's continuous phase lock on a satellite's signal. The coded pseudorange measurement is immune from this difficulty, but the carrier beat phase is not. In other words, even when a fixed double-difference solution can provide the correct integer ambiguity resolution, the moment the data set is interrupted by a cycle slip, that solution is lost.

There are actually two components to the carrier phase observable that ought not change from the moment of a receiver's lock onto a particular satellite. First is the fractional initial phase at the first moment of the lock. The receiver is highly unlikely to acquire the satellite's signal precisely at the beginning of a wavelength. It will grab on at some fractional part of a phase, and this fractional phase will remain unchanged for the duration of the observation. The other unchanged aspect of a normal carrier phase observable is an integer number of cycles. The integer cycle ambiguity is symbolized by N. It represents the number of full phase cycles between the receiver and the satellite at the first instant of the receiver's lock-on. The integer ambiguity ought to remain constant throughout an observation as well. But when there is a cycle slip, lock is lost, and by the time the receiver reacquires the signal, the normally constant integer ambiguity has changed.

Cycle Slip Causes

A power loss, a very low signal-to-noise ratio, a failure of the receiver software, a malfunctioning satellite oscillator, or any event that breaks the receiver's continuousreception of the satellite's signal causes a cycle slip. Most common, however, is an obstruction that is so solid it prevents the satellite signal from being tracked by the receiver. Under such circumstances, when the satellite reappears, the tracking resumes. The fractional phase may be the same as if tracking had been maintained, but the integer number of cycles is not.

Repairing Cycle Slips

Cycle slips are repaired in postprocessing. Both their location and their size must be determined; then the data set can be repaired with the application of a fixed quantity to all the subsequent phase observations. One approach is to hold the initial positions of the stations occupied by the receivers as fixed, and edit the data manually. This has proved to work, but would try the patience of Job. Another approach is to model the data on a satellite-dependent basis with continuous polynomials to find the breaks, and then manually edit the data set a few cycles at a time. In fact, several methods are available to find the lost integer phase value, but they all involve testing quantities.

One of the most convenient of these methods is based on the triple difference. It can provide an automated cycle slip detection system that is not confused by clock drift and, once least-squares convergence has been achieved, it can provide initial station positions, even using the unrepaired phase combinations. They may still contain cycle slips, but can nevertheless be used to process approximate baseline vectors. Then the residuals of these solutions are tested, sometimes through several iterations. Proceeding from its own station solutions, the triple difference can predict how many cycles will occur over a particular time interval. Therefore, by evaluating triple-difference residuals over that particular interval, it is not only possible to determine whichsatellites have integer jumps, but also the number of cycles that have actually been lost. In a sound triple-difference solution without cycle slips, the residuals are usually limited to fractions of a cycle. Only those containing cycle slips have residuals close to one cycle or larger. Once cycle slips are discovered, their correction can be systematic.

For example, suppose the residuals of one component double difference of a triple-difference solution revealed that the residual of satellite PRN 16 minus the residual of satellite PRN 17 was 8.96 cycles. Further suppose that the residuals from the second component double difference showed that the residual of satellite PRN 17 minus the residual of satellite PRN 20 was 14.04 cycles. Then one might remove 9 cycles from PRN 16 and 14 cycles from PRN 20 for all the subsequent epochs of the observation. However, the process might result in a common integer error for PRNS 16, 17, and 20. Still, small jumps of a couple of cycles can be detected and fixed in the double-difference solutions.

In other words, before attempting double difference solutions, the observations should be corrected for cycle slips identified from the triple difference solution. And even though small jumps undiscovered in the triple difference solution might remain in the data sets, the double difference residuals will reveal them at the epoch where they occurred.

However, some conditions may prevent the resolution of cycle slips down to the one-cycle level. Inaccurate satellite ephemerides, noisy data, errors in the receiver's initial positions, or severe ionospheric effects all can limit the effectiveness of cycle-slip fixing. In difficult cases, adetailed inspection of the residuals might be the best way to locate the problem.

Fixing the Integer Ambiguity and Obtaining Vector Solutions

When cycle slips have been finally eliminated, the ambiguities can be fixed to integer values. First, the standard deviations of the adjusted integers are inspected. If found to be significantly less than one cycle, they can be safely constrained to the nearest integer value. This procedure is only pertinent to double differences, since phase ambiguities are moot in triple differencing. The number of parameters involved can be derived by multiplying one, less the number of receivers by one, less the number of satellites involved in the observation. And for dual-frequency observations, the phase ambiguities for L1 and L2 are best fixed separately. But such a program of constraints is not typical in long baselines where the effects of the ionosphere and inaccuracies of the satellite ephemerides make the situation less determinable.

In small baselines, however, where these biases tend to be virtually identical at both ends, integer fixing is almost universal in GPS processing. Once the integer ambiguities of one baseline are fixed, the way is paved for constraint of additional ambiguities in subsequent iterations. Then, step by step, more and more integers are set, until all that can be fixed have been fixed. Baselines of several thousand kilometers can be constrained in this manner.

With the integer ambiguities fixed, the GPS observations produce a series of vectors, the rawmaterial for the final adjustment of the survey. The observed baselines represent very accurately determined relative locations between the stations they connect. However, the absolute position of the whole network is usually much less accurately known, although more accurate absolute positioning may be on the horizon for GPS. For now, there remains a considerable difference in the accuracy of relative and absolute positioning. A GPS survey is usually related to the rest of the world by translation of its Cartesian coordinates into ellipsoidal latitude, longitude, and height. Most users are less comfortable with the original coordinate results, given in the WGS84 coordinate system of the satellites themselves, than latitude, longitude, and height.

Adjustment

Least-Squares

There are numerous adjustment techniques, but least-squares adjustment is the most precise and most commonly used in GPS. The foundation of the idea of least-squares adjustment is the idea that the sum of the squares of all the residuals applied to the GPS vectors in their final adjustment should be held to the absolute minimum. But minimizing this sum requires first defining those residuals approximately. Therefore, in GPS it is based on equations where the observations are expressed as a function of unknown parameters, but parameters that are nonetheless given approximate initial values. This is the process that has been described above. Then by adding the squares of the terms thus formed and differentiating their sum, the derivatives can be set equal to zero. For complex work like GPS adjustments, matrix algebra is a valuabletool. The least-squares method has the advantage that it allows for the smallest possible changes to original estimated values.

The solution strategies of GPS adjustments themselves are best left to particular suites of software. Suffice it to say that the single baseline approach; that is, a baseline-by-baseline adjustment, has the disadvantage of ignoring the actual correlation of the observations of simultaneously occupied baselines. An alternative approach involves a network adjustment approach where the correlation between the baselines themselves can be more easily taken into account. And while the computations are simpler for the baseline-by-baseline approach, cycle slips are more conveniently repaired in network adjustment.

For the most meaningful network adjustment, the endpoints of every possible baseline should be connected to at least two other stations. Thereby, the quality of the work itself can be more realistically evaluated. For example, the most common observational mistake, the mismeasured antenna height, is very difficult to detect when adjusting baselines sequentially, one at a time, but a network solution spots such blunders more quickly.

Appendix

Land Surveying and Geomatics: On-line Resources
        http://homepage.interaccess.com/~maynard/index.html

Coast Guard -
        Bulletin Board
        (703) 313-5910
        8 data bits, 1 stop bit
        No parity, Full duplex
        XModem (CRC), 300/1200/2400 BPS

        Recorded Message
        (703) 313-5907

        Human
        (703) 313-5900

        Internet
        www.navcen.uscg.mil

NGS -
        Information Center
        (301) 713-3242

Federal Radionavigation Plan
        The National Technical Information Service
        Springfield, Virginia 22161
        Designation: DOT-VNTSC-RSPA-90-3/DOD-4650.4

Index